Amy Adams

countryside
softies

28 Handmade Wool Creatures to Stitch

stashBOOKS
an imprint of C&T Publishing

Text copyright © 2011 by Amy Adams

Artwork copyright © 2011 by C&T Publishing, Inc.

Publisher: Amy Marson

Creative Director: Gailen Runge

Acquisitions Editor: Susanne Woods

Editor: Liz Aneloski

Technical Editor: Sandy Peterson

Cover/Book Designer: Kristy Zacharias

Production Coordinator: Kirstie L. Pettersen

Production Editor: Julia Cianci

Illustrator: Kirstie L. Pettersen

Photography by Christina Carty-Francis and Diane Pedersen of C&T Publishing, Inc., unless otherwise noted

Published by Stash Books, an imprint of C&T Publishing, Inc., P.O. Box 1456, Lafayette, CA 94549

Library of Congress Cataloging-in-Publication Data

Adams, Amy (Amy Jane)

  Countryside softies : 28 handmade wool creatures to stitch / Amy Adams.

    p. cm.

  ISBN 978-1-60705-215-9 (softcover)

  1. Felt work. 2. Stuffed animals (Toys) 3. Soft toy making. I. Title.

  TT849.5.A325 2011

  746'.0463--dc22

                    2010028183

Printed in China

10 9 8 7 6 5 4 3 2 1

Dedication

To Alan—look what I did with your wooly jumpers!

In memory of Alan Pattinson 1923–2009

Acknowledgments

It's really hard to write this part of a book without sounding cheesy, but there are always certain special people who deserve a mention: my mum, my stepdad, my mother-in-law (who I get custody of should we ever divorce!), my two children, and my husband. Also to my friends who supported me through the stress when the box containing all of the finished softies for the book went missing on its way to America!

I must also acknowledge my fellow crafters, whom I meet with every day in the virtual design studio created around the water cooler of blogland—that is, Twitter.

A huge thank you to everyone at C&T Publishing, especially Susanne, Liz, Sandy, Julia, Diane, Christina, Kirstie, Kristy, and Megan.

contents

introduction

The patterns and instructions in this book are here to guide you through creating your very own whimsical softies in a few simple steps. A family of rabbits, a squirrel who has collected chestnuts, a toadstool, and a mother duck who lovingly has a chick and an egg tucked under her wings, to name a few, are ready and waiting to be brought to life. You will be more successful if you read the Basic Instructions before you start.

Each softie pattern is coded with a suggested level of expertise, ● **easy**, ●● **moderate**, or ●●● **slightly tricky**.

With a little time and small amounts of supplies, a soft toy, an ornament, or a commemorative gift materializes as if by magic. Many can be personalized by adding embroidery, or you can make a family group using the smaller patterns and accessories.

tip

As with any toy made for a small child, please exercise caution. Because of small parts, a softie may not be suitable for a child under the age of three.

what is a softie?

DEFINITION

Softie [sawf-tee, softy] – noun

1. A three-dimensional representation of a real or imaginary object, animal, or person re-created using soft materials.

2. Handmade using beautifully soft felted wool and gorgeous fabrics, resulting in exceptional cuteness.

Related words: plush, soft sculpture, soft toy, stuffed, stuffie, adorable!

basic instructions

getting started

Clear a little space to work in and familiarize yourself with the how-to section. Continue to refer back to these instructions when creating your softie. Many of them use the same techniques; once you have made one, the next will be much easier. The softies have been coded with a suggested level of sewing prowess. This is merely a guide, and all that ⦿⦿⦿ "slightly tricky" refers to is a larger project that has more parts to be sewn and will therefore take a bit longer to complete.

Gather your tools and materials. You will not need a huge stash of fabrics and threads; the projects are small and designed to be economical to put together while retaining an intimate and precious quality.

RECYCLE AND UPCYCLE

There can't be many crafters who are not inspired by the thrifty or recycling aspect that comes hand in hand with textiles. In the United Kingdom, we call it charity, and charity begins at home. Look no further than your and your family's closets.

Unwanted clothing can be pillaged for fabric, trims, and buttons and recycled (used again in its original state) and upcycled (used in a new and improved way, such as felting a wool sweater and making softies from it). There is no more wonderful feeling than turning a favorite outfit, once worn and loved by your growing child, into something else that will continue to be treasured.

BEGINNER VERSUS EXPERT

You do not need to be an expert with a needle to sew a softie. Felted wool and craft felt are very forgiving and can hide a multitude of sins. Even after your softie is complete, a quick squeeze here and there will help remedy any lumps or bumps that have appeared in the shape of the body. Using pearl cotton 8 for the appliqué and embroidery means your stitching stands out; it's meant to be seen. Odd stitches will look right at home. Give your softie a little of your own personality as the pattern transitions from the book into a truly individual creation, handmade by you!

tools and equipment

(Refer to Resources, page 140.)

SCISSORS

Use fabric shears for cutting out the fabrics and felt and embroidery scissors when sewing. Use a separate pair of paper scissors when cutting out the tracing paper patterns.

SEWING NEEDLES

The extra length and sturdiness of a darning needle is ideal when constructing a softie, while a smaller needle will be useful for attaching the small buttons.

PINS

Pins are vital for securing patterns and for things like ears, feet, wings, and tails, which are layered while cutting or sewing.

THIMBLE

A thimble is not essential, but it can be useful when stitching through some of the thicker parts of a softie.

AIR-ERASABLE FABRIC MARKER

Use one of these pens if you prefer to mark a guide before embroidering details.

PENCIL

This is used for tracing the patterns (pages 118–139) onto the tracing paper.

GLUESTICK

A gluestick will help secure the fabric strips in place that are used to cover the garden wire stem in several projects (page 10).

STUFFER STICK

Specific stuffer sticks are available to buy; however, a larger-sized knitting needle or even a chopstick will do the job of turning body parts right side out and getting the stuffing in the hard-to-reach areas.

SEWING MACHINE

A sewing machine is also not essential, but it will give stronger seams than hand sewing. If you choose to stitch the softie personalization (page 27) on a machine using free–motion stitching, you will need to be able to drop the feed dogs and attach a darning foot. Consult your machine's instruction booklet for how to do this.

WASHING MACHINE

Your washing machine will become your best friend when it comes to felting wool, but be nice to it. Remember to clean out the filter occasionally to remove any leftover fibers.

materials and notions *(Refer to Resources, page 140.)*

FELTED WOOL

The main ingredient for the softie patterns in this book is felted knitted wool (felted wool). This is something that can easily be produced at home with a few discarded woolens and a hot wash cycle in your washing machine (page 11).

CRAFT FELT

Craft felt comes in a selection of different fiber contents ranging from 100% acrylic to 100% wool. A felt with a 30% wool content has a lovely sheen, is very soft to work with, and is also economical. Since all the projects are quite small, only minimum quantities of craft felt will be needed—ideal for using up any scraps you have in your stash.

PRINTED FABRIC

Fabrics are an important part of the overall finished look and will really add personality. For most projects, just one printed cotton fabric will be fine, but you can use as many or as few as you like. As with the craft felt, small quantities are all you need. Recycle where you can, but if you'd like an excuse to go fabric shopping to add to your stash, then by all means, do!

SEWING THREAD

Sewing thread is used for constructing the softie's body; polyester thread is fine for this purpose.

EMBROIDERY THREAD

Most of the sewing beyond making the body parts is completed using pearl cotton 8. This thread will make a real feature of the appliqué and embroidery. A variegated thread (the color varies within the same spool) will add an extra dimension to your embroidery. In cases where a thicker thread is required, like for whiskers, pearl cotton 5 is ideal.

tip

As an alternative to pearl cotton thread, you could use three strands of embroidery floss.

INTERFACING

A heavyweight interfacing will help stabilize the craft felt during free-motion machine stitching and also strengthen the wings of the Butterfly (page 58) and Dragonfly (page 114).

BUTTONS

Mini buttons work best for eyes (page 17). In the crafting world, they are known as "micro mini rounds" or "tiny sew-thru shapes" and are about ¼″ (0.5cm) wide. For any additional buttons, pretty much anything will do. Don't be afraid to use pairs of buttons that don't match, as randomness adds to the softie's character.

A

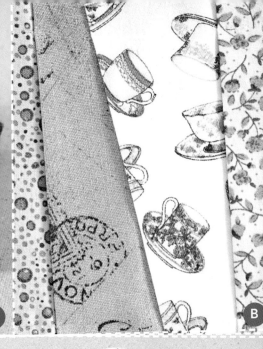

B

C

D

E

A. Felted wool

B. New printed fabrics

C. Recycled printed fabrics taken from old clothing

D. Embroidery thread

E. Buttons

STUFFING

There are two main types of stuffing available, natural (wool) or synthetic (polyester); which one you choose is a personal preference. A natural stuffing gives a nice, solid shape, and a synthetic one will be softer and lighter.

Natural fiber (wool) stuffing

Synthetic (polyester) stuffing

FRAY CHECK

The printed fabric used is finished with a raw edge and a blanket or straight stitch. While I prefer the fabric to be left alone so it frays slightly, if you have any concerns about this, dab a small amount of Fray Check on the fabric edges to seal them.

CARD STOCK

Any softie that sits upright will need a level base for balance. Popping an oval of card stock inside the base does the trick. Cardboard from an empty cereal box also has an ideal thickness.

TRACING PAPER

Trace the patterns on tracing paper or a thin drawing paper. This way you can get started straight away rather than having to visit your local copy shop.

PEBBLES

There are many ways to weight a softie. A pebble or small stone from your own garden, placed in the base, works really well, since the size and shape can be chosen to match the softie. Or you can use a small quantity of rice or lentils.

GARDEN WIRE

Use a heavyweight wire (strong enough to bend and hold its shape, but easy to cut to length) for the Bulrush/Cattail stems (page 113) and the Squirrel's tail (page 67).

felting wool

The best source of wool suitable for felting at home is old clothes. Sweaters, cardigans, scarves—any garment will do, as long as it is made from knitted wool.

NOTE

You can use woven wool in theory, and although it does felt up nicely, it doesn't give quite the same cuddly effect when made up into a softie. It also doesn't have the same give as knitted wool, so it is harder to stuff and shape.

What you are looking for is a high wool content, 70% or above, and with "hand wash" on the label. Something that is a soft, fine knit is ideal. If it's too thick, it will be difficult to sew after it's felted. Cotton or anything synthetic (such as acrylic or polyester) will not felt. However, no more than 30% of these fibers mixed with at least 70% wool will be fine. Also, watch out for wool labeled as "superwash." Superwash wool has been chemically treated to protect it from felting, although if you mistreat it enough in your washing machine, it will give in to the process, eventually!

Some wools felt fine after just one wash; others will need two or even three wash cycles. Felting is not an exact science. What you are looking for is a fluffiness to the surface and a little bit of shrinkage. Check the felting process by making a small cut in the garment. If the knitting looks like it would still unravel, then go through the process again.

Follow these steps to felt knitted wool:

1. Remove any buttons or trims and then place the item (or items) in the washing machine. You can felt 2 or 3 garments at the same time. Use your everyday detergent and run a hot wash cycle.

2. Let the garments air dry.

3. Make a small cut on one of the sleeves to check that it's properly felted.

4. Repeat Steps 1–3 again if need be.

Before felting; the knit is still visible.

After felting; the knit is now fused.

You can see in the before and after images that the difference is quite subtle. After you've felted a couple of times, you will begin to be able to tell how well a garment will felt from experience.

tip

The felted wool gives a lovely soft and cuddly finish to the softies, but any of the projects will work if made entirely out of woven fabrics.

making a softie

Refer to the basic techniques in the following sections when making softies following the project instructions. Everything you need to know is here.

FELTED WOOL, CRAFT FELT, AND PRINTED FABRICS

Fabric and felt color is not specified in the project instructions; it's your choice. Realistic color has been used, where possible, to demonstrate each softie, but don't feel that you have to do the same. Let your imagination guide you; experiment and be bold. *The quantities given in each pattern are pretty generous, so you shouldn't run out mid-project.*

CUTTING OUT THE PIECES

All of the patterns are *actual size* and will only require enlarging (as would the suggested felt and fabric quantities) if you want to be really adventurous and make a larger softie. *Seam allowances are included but not shown on the patterns.*

1. Trace the patterns (pages 118–139) onto tracing paper, including any additional markings, and cut them out.

2. Pin all of the traced and cut patterns required onto the right side of a single layer of the felted wool, printed fabric, or craft felt to make sure they all fit *before* cutting them out.

3. Cut out the pieces.

NOTES

All fabrics have a right side and a wrong side. Even craft felt will have a slightly smoother side, which should be classed as the right side. Some of the patterns are not symmetrical and will require flipping before cutting a second piece. Each of the individual instructions contains a reminder if this is the case.

Right sides together or wrong sides together? As a general rule of thumb for making any of the softies: their parts that are to be stitched and then turned so the seam is on the inside will start out life *right sides together*. Any parts stitched around the edge using a blanket stitch (page 22) will begin with the *wrong sides together*.

Patterns do not need to be cut with 100% accuracy. Making a softie is a much more organic process than some other crafts; there is a little leeway. Because of the thickness of the felted wool, it will be easier to cut a smidgen away from the edge of the pattern than to try to stick to it exactly.

MAKING BODIES

Stitching

1. Pin the 2 main body pieces right sides together.

2. Stitch just less than ¼″ (0.5cm) in from the edge with a general sewing thread in a matching color. Stitch either by hand using a backstitch (page 23) or on a sewing machine using a straight stitch (page 26), backstitching at the beginning and end. Leave the turning gap open. While machine sewing is not essential, it will make the project quicker and result in stronger stitching.

Stitching done in white for visibility. When you stitch, use thread color to match felted wool.

3. Turn the body right side out.

Stuffing and Molding

Adding the stuffing is an important part of the process, since this is what bridges the gap between the two-dimensional and the three-dimensional stages.

Push small pieces of stuffing in place, using the stuffer stick for the harder-to-reach areas (page 7). Fill the smaller areas first, moving on to the main body section, which can be filled with larger handfuls of stuffing.

The softies can take more stuffing than you expect and work best when given a more solid appearance. As you go, keep turning the softie right side up to check the shape for any lumps and bumps. Treat this process like you are molding clay, until you have a body shape you are happy with. If it's not going well, just take the stuffing out and start again. It's worthwhile taking your time to get it right before the base is stitched on.

NOTE

A seam allowance is included within each pattern. Stitching an exact seam allowance is not necessary, so stitch just less than ¼″, or about 0.5cm, in from the edge. There is a small gap annotated on each body pattern where required. This is the hole through which the body will be turned right side out, hiding all seams on the inside, and where the stuffing is inserted. All softies will look a little smaller at this stage, but the felted wool has a fair amount of give and can take quite a bit of stuffing, which allows the shape to grow.

Weighting and Adding the Base

1. Make a small well in the stuffing in the base.

2. Select a pebble that is a suitable size and shape and wrap a little extra stuffing around it to soften any sharp edges or roughness. (figure A)

3. Insert the pebble and add some more stuffing on top of it.

4. Cut an oval piece of card stock to size, using the measurements included in the project instructions. It can be just a roughly cut oval, although do trim the size and shape if it's too big.

5. Place the card-stock base in the body cavity, so it lies flat. (figure B)

6. Place the felted-wool base on top of the card-stock base and the open gap. Using a length of pearl cotton 8 thread, knot the thread to begin sewing on the inside of the body and stitch in place using random straight stitches (page 23). Once the base is sewn in place, bring the needle up through the body to where the tummy patch will sit, so you can continue stitching with the same thread. (figure C)

figure A | Use 2 or more pebbles for larger softies to create a sturdy base to allow the softie to stand up without toppling over.

figure B

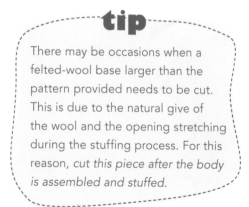

tip

There may be occasions when a felted-wool base larger than the pattern provided needs to be cut. This is due to the natural give of the wool and the opening stretching during the stuffing process. For this reason, *cut this piece after the body is assembled and stuffed.*

figure C

countryside **softies**

ADDING TUMMY AND CHEST PATCHES

Stitch the printed-fabric tummy or chest patches to the body with random straight stitches (page 23) using pearl cotton 8.

tip

At this point, if you need to begin with a fresh length of thread, position the knot underneath the tummy or chest patch, so it is hidden.

Some tummy and chest patches will require an added tuck or dart to allow the fabric to follow the body shape more closely. In the case of some of the birds (see the Duck, page 102), the chest patch extends down to also cover the base of the softie. With the Otter (page 94) and Fox (page 30), the chest patch is placed higher up, toward the face. This is to allow the fabric underside of the snout to line up with the chest area. These points are all noted within the individual project instructions.

MAKING SNOUTS AND BEAKS

The Otter (page 94) and the Fox (page 30) both have snouts. A snout is made up of a printed-fabric underside and a felted-wool top. The beaks for both the Swan (page 98) and the Duck (page 102) are completed and attached in very much the same way as a snout.

1. Pin the 2 snout/beak shapes right sides together and stitch, just less than ¼˝ (0.5cm) in from the edge, with a general sewing thread in a matching color, either by hand using a backstitch (page 23) or on a sewing machine using a straight stitch (page 26). Leave the edge that attaches to the face open.

2. Turn the snout/beak right side out, so the seam is now on the inside.

3. Use a stuffer stick to poke out any points and fill with a little stuffing.

4. Hold the snout/beak in position on the softie's face, lining up the underside of the snout/beak with the top edge of the fabric chest area (if applicable). Pin and then attach it, using random straight stitches (page 23) in pearl cotton 8, catching both the softie's body and the snout with each stitch.

Attach snout using random straight stitches.

The beaks for the Robin (page 48), Owls (page 76), and the Kingfisher (page 108) are simpler, requiring just a piece of craft felt cut to size and attached with random straight stitches using pearl cotton 8.

ADDING EYES

1. Bring the thread up in position for the first eye. Add one of the craft-felt circles and then a mini button and bring the thread back through the circle and into the stuffed face.

2. Take the needle to the correct position for the second eye and repeat.

ADDING MOUTHS

The Squirrel (page 64), Rabbits (page 34), and the Hedgehogs (page 42) have embroidered mouths. Stitch a few backstitches (page 23), using pearl cotton 8, in the shape of a small vertical line, with a smile shape across the base.

MAKING EARS

Ears all consist of a felted-wool back and a printed-fabric front.

1. Pin 2 ear pieces wrong sides together. Stitch around the edges with a blanket stitch (page 22), using pearl cotton 8. Anchor the thread with a knot between the 2 layers, so it is hidden, and leave the bottom of the ear open.

2. Attach each ear to the softie using random straight stitches (page 23). On one side of the ear, sew each straight stitch through the softie and also through the printed-fabric layer. Do the same on the other side of the ear, catching the felted-wool layer and the body. Some of the ears are folded at the bottom, but they are still attached using random straight stitches.

Front of Fox's ear

Back of Fox's ear

MAKING WINGS

Some of the wings are attached using the same technique as for the ears (page 17), sewing random straight stitches on both layers. This is the case with the Butterfly (page 58) and the Dragonfly (page 114). For the Robin (page 48), Owls (page 76), Swan (page 98), Duck (page 102), and Kingfisher (page 108), the wings are stitched all the way around the edge in a blanket stitch (page 22) using pearl cotton 8, and then fixed in place on each side of the softie using a button.

MAKING FEET/CLAWS AND ARMS

All are completed in more or less the same way.

1. Pin 2 pieces wrong sides together. Stitch around the edge using a blanket stitch (page 22) with pearl cotton 8, anchoring the thread with a starting knot in between the 2 layers, so it is hidden. Leave a small gap—about 1″ (2.5cm) on the edge—as you stitch close to the beginning stitches.

2. Add a little stuffing inside and continue with the blanket stitch to close the gap. Instructions within each project cover any additional detailing embroidery.

3. To attach the foot, thread the needle with pearl cotton 8, anchoring the thread with a knot on the body underneath where the foot will sit, so the knot is hidden. Place the back of the foot in position against the body and bring the needle up through the bottom layer only of the foot at position 1 (as indicated in the diagram below). Take the needle about ½″ (1cm) forward inside the foot and then bring it back out at position 2, and then down into the body at position 3. Take the needle ⅓″ (1cm) forward inside the body this time, then out at position 4, and back up into the foot at position 5. Continue to do this, weaving the thread in and out, a little bit like the ladder stitch, between the limb and the body until you have gone all the way around, pulling the thread taut as you go, so it is secure.

— Thread inside
— Thread between 2 body parts

Body —

1
2
3
4
5

— Limb to be attached

The same technique is used to attach the Carrot to the Rabbit's body (page 41), the Fish to the Otter's arms, and the Otter's tail to its body where it curls (page 96).

The Otter's arms are attached slightly differently. Hold them in position, pin, and stitch directly onto the body, using a button at each shoulder.

MAKING TAILS

Most tails consist of a felted-wool layer and a printed-fabric layer.

Pin the pieces wrong sides together and stitch around the edge in a blanket stitch (page 22), using the pearl cotton 8. Attach the tail to the softie's body with a single button.

The exceptions include the Rabbits (pages 34 and 38), which have a pompom or a heart shape; the Squirrel (page 64), which has a fringed tail; and the Baby Mouse (page 86), whose tail is created using a small length of wool yarn. The Otter's tail (page 96) is also made slightly differently, as it is stuffed and attached with random straight stitches.

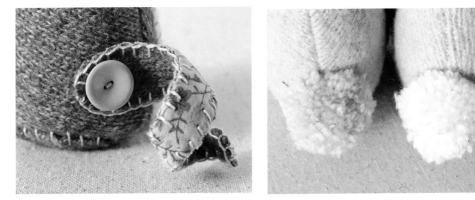

MAKING WHISKERS, INSECT LEGS, AND ANTENNAE

1. Thread a needle with 4˝ (10cm) of pearl cotton 5. (This thread is slightly thicker than pearl cotton 8.)

2. These features are all created in pairs. Take the needle in on one side of the softie, where the first whisker, leg, or antenna starts; push the needle straight through to the other side and out where the second appendage starts. Remove the needle and tie a knot near the beginning end of the thread. Gently pull on the other end until the first whisker, leg, or antenna is the required length. Tie another knot near the other end, even with the first, and trim off any excess thread.

3. Repeat this procedure to add more. The whiskers, legs, or antennae will be able to move about, so the length on each side can be adjusted, but the knot will prevent them from being completely removed.

TYING-OFF THREADS

When you have finished sewing or need to add a fresh length of thread, tie off by taking the needle to a place where it will be hidden, behind a foot or underneath a wing for example. Make 3 or 4 stitches on the same spot and then take the needle through the body of the softie and out the other side. Gently pull the thread, snip off the visible end, and the end will disappear safely back within the body.

NOTES

- All finished sizes represent width and height, *with the smallest measurement coming first*. These are a rough guide, as finished sizes will vary slightly depending on the stuffing process and how much give the felted wool has.

- Refer to photographs and illustrations for positioning of limbs, ears, eyes, facial features, and so forth.

- Unless otherwise directed, use pearl cotton 8 for all appliqué and embroidery.

- When pinning 2 pieces together, take note from the instructions whether to pin them *right sides* together or *wrong sides* together. The rule of thumb for this is that if a piece is to be turned inside out, so any seams are on the inside, then begin with right sides together. If it is sewn with a blanket stitch as a decorative-edged seam, then begin with wrong sides together.

- Additional body parts, such as ears and feet, do not need to be in the same shade of felted wool. As long as they coordinate, you can mix and match to make use of smaller, leftover pieces from other projects.

- Add a flower to any of the patterns to make your softie female.

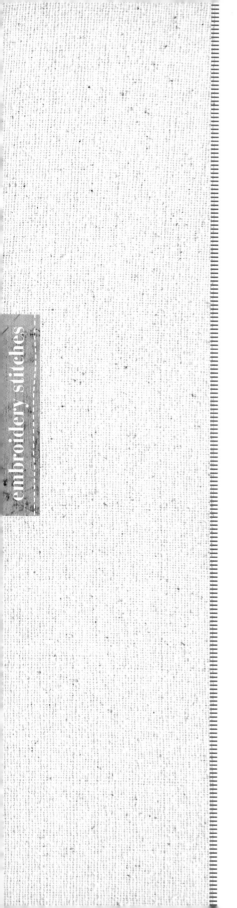
embroidery stitches

HAND SEWING

Blanket Stitch

This is a decorative edging stitch used to join layers of printed fabric and felt.

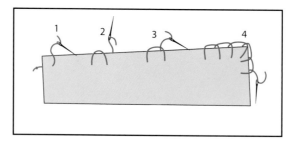

1. Bring the threaded needle through to the front from between the 2 layers, ¼″ (0.5cm) from the fabric edge, so a knot can be trapped inside to anchor it [1].

2. Move ¼″ (0.5cm) horizontally from the needle's entry point and insert the needle again, through both layers, to the back. Pull through to form a small loop at the front [2]. You can work either to the right or left, whichever feels comfortable.

3. Thread the needle through this loop and gently pull, not too tight, for the first stitch [3]; your last stitch will need to link in to it when you have stitched all the way around.

4. Continue blanket stitching all around the edge by repeating Steps 2 and 3. For a corner, make a stitch at 45° and then turn the piece you are sewing [4], since it is easier to sew horizontally, and continue.

5. To end, take the needle through the loop of your first stitch and pull tight. To tie off, take small stitches through the layers a couple of times more to anchor. Then bring the needle a few lengths through the middle of both layers and out one side. Gently pull and trim off any excess.

Straight Stitch

This stitch is used in a decorative way to attach appliqué patches of printed fabric to the softie.

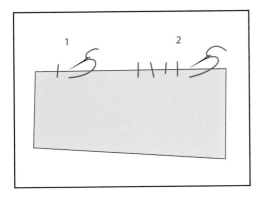

1. Attach the thread to the softie so the knot will be hidden underneath the appliqué patch. Place the patch on the softie, and either pin it in place if it's a larger patch or just hold it in place if it's small.

2. Bring the needle up through the printed fabric close to the edge.

3. Take the needle back down into just the softie, making a stitch ¼″ (0.5cm) in length. With the same motion, bring the needle back up through both the softie and the printed fabric, roughly ¼″ (0.5cm) away from the first exit point [1].

4. Repeat Step 3 until you have gone all the way around [2]. The stitches do not need to be equal. A bit of randomness adds to the uniqueness of the design. Secure the last stitch (see Tying-Off Threads, page 20).

Backstitch

Backstitches give a continuous line of thread, ideal if you are making your softie by hand and also for stitching any lettering and the facial expressions.

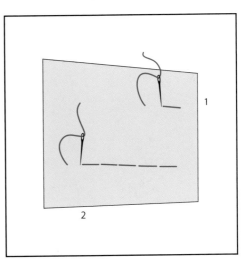

1. Bring the needle through to the surface of the base you are stitching on.

2. Take a small stitch backward through the base, bringing the needle up about a stitch's length ahead of the current stitch. Gently pull the thread taut.

3. Insert the needle backward into the base next to the stitch you just completed [1] and bring the needle up a stitch's length in front of the current stitch.

4. Repeat Step 3 until the stitched line is complete [2]. Secure the last stitch (see Tying-Off Threads, page 20).

Running Stitch

This is an ideal stitch for joining two or more layers of fabric or felt and also for gathering (used for the Chestnut, page 70).

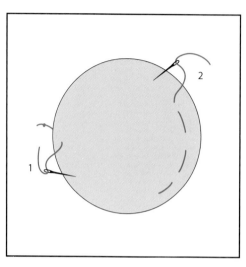

1. Bring the needle through to the surface [1] in the required position and then back down, creating a stitch of ¼″ (0.5cm) in length [2].

2. Leaving a small gap between each stitch, repeat Step 1.

3. Secure the thread in place (see Tying-Off Threads, page 20) for a simple line of running stitch or gently pull the loose end of the thread for gathering, as directed.

French Knot

This is a useful knotted stitch for embroidered lettering and other embellishments.

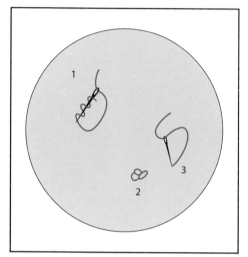

1. Bring the needle through to the surface in the required position and wrap the thread around the needle 2 or 3 times, depending on the size knot you want [1].

2. Insert the needle back through, close to where it first emerged, and gently pull until the knotted thread settles in place [2].

3. Secure the thread in place for a single knot (see Tying-Off Threads, page 20) or move to the next position to continue the embroidery [3].

Fly Stitch

This is a useful and decorative embroidery stitch.

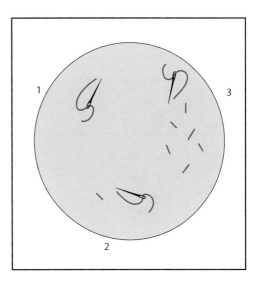

1. Bring the needle through to the surface of the base you are stitching on, insert the needle ¼″ (0.5cm) away, and pull the thread, leaving a small loop [1].

2. Insert the needle again, centered and a little below the initial entry points. Run the thread through the loop and make a small downward stitch to hold it in place, so it forms the shape of the letter Y [2].

3. Secure the thread in place for a single stitch (see Tying-Off Threads, page 20) or move to the next position to continue the embroidery [3].

Seed Stitch

These are miniature straight stitches used for embroidered decoration.

1. Bring the needle up at the desired start point [1].

2. Insert the needle again just a short distance away and either secure the thread in place for a single stitch (see Tying-Off Threads, page 20) or move to the next position to continue [2].

3. Vary the direction and size of the stitches to give a random pattern when filling an area with seed stitch [3].

Whipstitch

Use this for an easy way of closing the gap once a softie is stuffed.

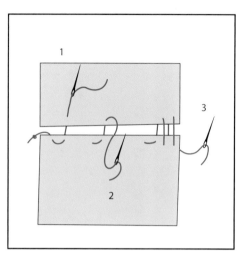

1. Thread the needle with sewing thread that matches the body color and tie a knot in the end.

2. Bring the needle up through the fabric from within the open gap, so the knot is hidden on the inside.

3. Tuck both fabric edges of the gap inward (not shown) and pinch together with your fingers to hold them in place. Then pass the needle through both layers, pulling the thread all the way through [1].

4. Bring the needle back to the first side [2], so the thread sits over the top, and again pass the needle through both layers, pulling the thread all the way through. Repeat until the gap is closed [3].

MACHINE SEWING

Straight Stitch

This is the most basic of all the sewing-machine stitches. When sewing softies, make sure both the top thread and the bobbin thread are the same color and remember to clean out underneath the stitch plate occasionally, since the felted wool will leave fibers behind.

Zigzag Stitch

Another simple stitch for softies, the zigzag can be used to trap the garden wire within the layers of felted wool, such as when making the Squirrel's tail (page 67).

Free-Motion Machine Stitching

This is a speedy way to stitch a personalization using letters of the alphabet.

1. Drop the feed dogs on your sewing machine; there will be a lever or button to accomplish this. (Refer to your machine's instruction booklet.) Attach a darning foot and set the machine to a normal straight stitch.

2. If you want to draw guidelines to stitch on, use the air-erasable fabric marker. Place a piece of interfacing underneath the craft felt to stabilize it.

3. Using the hand wheel, slowly bring the needle down through the craft felt and back up again. Pull the top thread to expose the bobbin thread and bring the bobbin thread through the fabric to the surface. This keeps it from getting tangled underneath as you stitch.

4. Slowly begin sewing, gently moving the fabric around so you are literally drawing with the needle. You may need to go over the lettering twice to make it clear, and don't be afraid to stop and jump from one word to the next, since any unwanted threads will be trimmed off.

5. When you have finished, trim loose and unwanted threads and any excess interfacing.

free machine embroidery

tip

Many sewing machines come with preset alphabets, but I find it is much more personal to stitch your own handwriting.

in the
hedgerow

During my days as a counted cross-stitch designer, many of the designs undertaken were illustrative scenes of nature. The fox was one of the most popular animals to feature. Their mysterious yet appealing character captures the imagination, which is why they remain popular among softie makers too.

You will need

- 1 piece 8˝ × 14˝ (20cm × 35cm) of felted wool (page 8) for body, ears, snout, feet, tail, and base

- 1 piece 5˝ × 5½˝ (12.5cm × 14cm) of printed fabric for chest patch and snout

- 1 piece 2˝ × 4˝ (5cm × 10cm) of printed fabric for ears

- 1 piece 4˝ × 6˝ (10cm × 15cm) of printed fabric for feet and tail

- 1 piece 4˝ × 6˝ (10cm × 15cm) of printed fabric also for feet and tail

- 1 piece 1˝ × 2˝ (2.5cm × 5cm) of craft felt for eyes

- 2 mini buttons for eyes

- 2 buttons for nose and attaching tail

- 1 oval of card stock 1½˝ × 2˝ (3.5cm × 5cm) for base

- 1 pebble for weight

- Stuffing

- A selection of coordinating pearl cotton 8 threads for appliqué and embroidery

- Sewing thread in a color to match the body parts, suitable for use either in a sewing machine or for hand stitching, for constructing the Fox

Read the Basic Instructions (pages 6–27) for more detailed information.

Patterns are on pages 118–119. Trace and cut out the patterns.

- If you don't have 4 different but coordinating printed fabrics available, 2 will work fine; make the ears, tail, and feet with just 1 printed fabric. The Fox will look best if the chest and snout are different from the ears, feet, and tail.

- You may need to experiment with different buttons for the nose; select one that gives your Fox a quirky character.

BODY

1. From the felted wool, cut the following: 2 bodies, 1 base, 2 ears, 2 feet, 1 snout, and 1 tail.

2. Construct the body (pages 13–14). Stuff it and add the pebble for weight. Add the card-stock base and attach the felted-wool base.

3. From the first printed fabric, cut the chest patch and sew it in place (page 15), making sure the curve in the top section follows the shape of the Fox's head.

SNOUT, EARS, AND EYES

1. From the first printed fabric, cut 1 snout.

2. Construct the snout using a felted-wool piece and the printed-fabric piece (pages 15–16) and attach it to the face, with the printed fabric on the underside.

3. Add a button nose and a few straight stitches (page 23) for nose wrinkles, in either the same color or a darker color thread.

4. From the second printed fabric, cut 2 ears.

5. Construct the ears using a felted-wool piece and a printed-fabric piece (page 17, wrong sides together, using the blanket stitch, and attach them to the head.

6. From craft felt, cut 2 eye circles and attach them with the mini buttons (page 17).

FEET

1. Place the third and fourth printed fabrics right sides together and sew along one long edge using a ¼″ (0.5cm) seam allowance. Open the printed-fabric unit and press. Then cut 2 foot shapes (making sure you leave enough fabric to cut out the tail), lining up the join line on the pattern with the fabric seam.

2. For each foot, pair up a printed-fabric unit and a felted-wool piece, pinned wrong sides together.

3. On one foot, sew a blanket stitch all the way around, leaving the bottom straight edge open. Fill the foot with a little stuffing and continue with the blanket stitch to close up the gap. Add 2 or 3 backstitch lines, about ¾″ (2cm) long, to create toes. Repeat for the other foot and then attach both feet in place on the body (page 18).

TAIL

1. On the printed-fabric unit (see Feet, above), position the tail pattern upside down from the direction you used to cut out the tail piece from the felted wool. Line up the join mark on the pattern with the seam between the 2 fabrics and cut out a tail. Pin the fabric to the felted-wool tail, wrong sides together, and sew a blanket stitch all the way around the edge.

2. Just stitching through the top printed-fabric layer, add 3 embroidered crosses, made up of 2 straight stitches each, to decorate the seam between the printed fabrics.

3. Attach the tail, fabric side facing forward, to the rear of the body, using the remaining button.

rabbit

Finished size
Male: approximately 8¾″ × 4½″ (22cm × 11cm), including the ears and tail
Female: approximately 8½″ × 4½″ (21cm × 11cm), including the ears and tail

One of my daughter's favorite storybooks is *Little Rabbit Lost,* by Harry Horse, a whimsical tale of a rabbit family and the birthday adventure experienced by the littlest rabbit. With this in mind, what began as a single rabbit pattern evolved into a whole warren that hops around the hedges of the farmers' fields, naughtily nibbling at the crop of carrots.

You will need

(Makes 1 adult male or female)

- 1 piece 10″ × 12″ (25cm × 30cm) of felted wool (page 8) for body, ears, feet, and base

- 1 piece 3½″ × 4½″ (9cm × 11cm) of felted wool for feet

- 1 piece 5″ × 8″ (12.5cm × 20cm) of printed fabric for tummy patch and ears

- 1 piece 1″ × 2″ (2.5cm × 5cm) of craft felt for eyes

- 5½ yards (5m) of wool yarn for pompom

- 2 mini buttons for eyes

- 1 button for nose

- 1 oval of card stock 1¼″ × 2″ (3cm × 5cm) for base

- 2 circles 1½″ (3.5cm) in diameter of card stock, with a hole ½″ (1.25cm) in diameter cut out of the center, for pompom

- 1 pebble for weight

- Stuffing

- A selection of coordinating pearl cotton 8 threads for the appliqué and embroidery

- White pearl cotton 5 thread for whiskers

- Sewing thread in a color to match the body parts, suitable for use either in a sewing machine or for hand stitching, for constructing the Rabbit

Additional for a female Rabbit:
- 2″ × 2″ (5cm × 5cm) square of craft felt and 1 button for flower

Additional for a male Rabbit:
- 1″ × 2½″ (2.5cm × 6.5cm) rectangle of craft felt for tie

Read the Basic Instructions (pages 6–27) for more detailed information.

Patterns are on pages 120–121. Trace and cut out the patterns.

BODY

1. From the felted wool, cut the following, using either the male or female adult Rabbit patterns: 2 bodies (1 and 1 reverse), 1 base, 2 feet, and 2 ears.

2. Construct the body (pages 13–14). Stuff it and add the pebble for weight. Add the card-stock base and attach the felted-wool base.

3. From the printed fabric, cut 1 tummy patch and 2 ears. Sew the tummy patch in place (page 15).

EARS AND FEET

1. Construct the ears using a felted-wool piece and a printed-fabric piece (page 17), wrong sides together, using a blanket stitch. Fold the bottom of the sides of the ears into the center and attach them to the head.

2. Cut 2 more feet from the second felted wool for the backs of the feet. Sort the felted-wool feet into pairs (a front with a back) and pin each set wrong sides together. Construct a foot (page 18) using a blanket stitch. Add a couple of vertical backstitch lines, about ¾" (2cm) long, to create toes. Repeat for the other foot and then attach both feet in place on the body.

FACE

1. From craft felt, cut 2 eye circles and attach them using the mini buttons (page 8). Also attach the button nose and add the whiskers (page 20) and a mouth (page 17).

2. For a female Rabbit, cut the additional craft-felt square into a flower and attach it to the head using a button. For a male Rabbit, cut the additional craft-felt rectangle into a tie and attach it to the front of the neck with 2 crossed straight stitches, using pearl cotton 8.

TAIL

Using the card-stock circles and the wool yarn, make a pompom (below) and stitch it in place on the body.

Making a Pompom

1. Cut the wool into manageable lengths and thread a length onto a needle. Placing the 2 circles of card stock together, begin to wrap the wool yarn around the card by threading it through the central hole. Keep doing so, working your way around the ring, until all the card stock is covered. Each time a length of wool yarn runs out, there is no need to tie on a new piece. Just make sure all the loose ends lie on the outer edge of the ring.

2. Once there is no space in the center to thread wool yarn through, cut around the outer edge, through all the wool, so the scissor blades pass between the pieces of card stock. Thread an additional small length of wool yarn between the card-stock rings. Pulling tightly, tie it firmly in place and remove the card stock by tearing it away. Fluff the pompom and finish it off by trimming any excess wool yarn to tidy up the pompom shape.

baby rabbit

Finished size approximately 3″ × 6″ (7.5cm × 15cm), including the ears and tail

You will need

(Makes 1 male or female)

- 1 piece 8″ × 10″ (20cm × 25cm) piece of felted wool (page 8) for body, ears, and base

- 1 piece 6″ × 6″ (15cm × 15cm) of printed fabric for ears and tummy patch

- 1 piece 1″ × 2″ (2.5cm × 5cm) of craft felt for eyes

- 2 squares 2″ × 2″ (5cm × 5cm) of craft felt for tail

- 1 piece 2″ × 2″ (5cm × 5cm) of heavyweight interfacing for tail (optional)

- 2 mini buttons for eyes

- 1 button for nose

- 1 oval of card stock 1″ × 1¾″ (2.5cm × 4cm) for base

- 1 pebble for weight

- Stuffing

- A selection of coordinating pearl cotton 8 threads for the appliqué and embroidery

- White pearl cotton 5 thread for the whiskers

tips

- If you are making more than one Rabbit, the felted wool does not all have to be the same color. The colors can vary for each, and can vary for the base, feet, and ears, which is ideal for using up scraps.

- Use the printed fabrics you select to help depict a male or female Rabbit.

- Anything can be embroidered onto the Baby Rabbits' tails, for example, a name and birth date or a simple "Hello" greeting.

- Use the patterns to create your own uniquely personal family group.

- Sewing thread in a color to match the body parts, suitable for use either in a sewing machine or for hand stitching, for constructing the Baby Rabbit

Additional for a female Baby Rabbit:
- 1 piece 1½″ × 1½″ (3.5cm × 3.5cm) of craft felt and 1 button for flower

Additional for a male Baby Rabbit:
- 1 piece 2″ × 3″ (5cm × 7.5cm) of rust or orange craft felt for Carrot

- 2 pieces ½″ × 1½″ (1.5cm × 3.5cm) of green craft felt for Carrot top

Read the Basic Instructions (pages 6–27) for more detailed information.

Patterns are on page 122. Trace and cut out the patterns.

BODY

1. From the felted wool, cut 2 bodies (1 and 1 reverse), 1 base, and 2 ears.

2. Construct the body (pages 13–14). Stuff it and add the pebble for weight. Add the card-stock base and attach the felted-wool base.

3. From the printed fabric, cut 1 tummy patch and 2 ears. Sew the tummy patch in place (page 15).

EARS

Construct the ears using a felted-wool piece and a printed-fabric piece (page 17), wrong sides together, with a blanket stitch. Fold the bottom of the sides into the center and attach them to the head.

FACE

1. From craft felt, cut 2 eye circles and attach them with the mini buttons (page 8). Also attach the button nose and add the whiskers (page 20) and a mouth (page 17).

2. For a female Baby Rabbit, cut the additional craft-felt square into a flower and attach it to the head using a button.

TAIL

1. From craft felt, cut 2 heart shapes. To personalize, on 1 of the heart shapes mark the lettering, if need be, and then embroider either in a backstitch using the pearl cotton 8 (page 23) or via free-motion machine stitching (page 27). If you're using free-motion embroidery, place a heart shape of interfacing underneath the felt to strengthen it. (The interfacing only needs to be used if you're using a sewing machine. It's not needed for hand sewing, as it would be too stiff to stitch through.)

2. Trim off any excess interfacing if used. Pin the embroidered heart to the other blank heart and sew a blanket stitch (page 22) around the edge to join them, adding a little stuffing inside as you go.

3. Stitch the heart-shaped tail in place on the body (page 19).

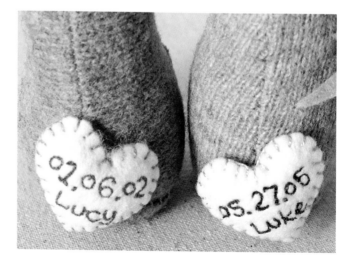

carrot

1. For a male Baby Rabbit, make a Carrot and attach it to the side of the body. From the rust or orange craft felt, cut 2 Carrot shapes and roughly cut each of the 2 green pieces into a small, long triangle shape about ¼˝ × 1⅜˝ (0.6cm × 3.5cm).

2. Pin the craft-felt Carrot pieces together and sew a blanket stitch (page 22) around the edge, leaving a gap of ½˝ (1.5cm) at the top. Through this gap, push in a little stuffing. Tuck in the green triangles so most of them is still poking out. Continue to sew a blanket stitch to close the gap, trapping in the green felt as you go. Add a bit of detailing to the Carrot body with a few backstitched (page 23) horizontal lines.

hedgehog

Finished size approximately 3″ × 6″ (7.5cm × 15cm)

One lazy summer's day, after collecting my children from school, I was in the kitchen preparing tea when something moving caught my eye. Just beyond the back door was a hedgehog in our garden. Next to this hedgehog was an even smaller hedgehog, a tiny baby. We sat watching them through the glass until they disappeared back under the shed where they live. That was the first year we saw them, and we've had hedgehogs every summer since.

You will need

- 2 pieces 5″ × 5″ (12.5cm × 12.5cm) of felted wool (page 8) for body

- 1 piece 3″ × 3″ (7.5cm × 7.5cm) of felted wool (page 8) for base

- 1 piece 4″ × 10″ (10cm × 25cm) of felted wool (page 8) for spines

- 2 pieces 5″ × 5″ (12.5cm × 12.5cm) of printed fabric for body (face)

- 1 piece 1″ × 2″ (2.5cm × 5cm) of craft felt for eyes

- 2 mini buttons for eyes

- 1 button for nose

- 1 oval of card stock 1½″ × 2″ (3.5cm × 5cm) for base

- 1 pebble for weight

- Stuffing

- A selection of coordinating pearl cotton 8 threads for the appliqué and embroidery

- Sewing thread in a color to match the body parts, suitable for use either in a sewing machine or for hand stitching, for constructing the Hedgehog

Additional for a female Hedgehog:
- 2″ × 2″ (5cm × 5cm) square of craft felt and 1 button for flower

Read the Basic Instructions (pages 6–27) for more detailed information.

Patterns are on page 123. Trace and cut out the patterns.

tips

- The printed fabrics you select will help distinguish between a male and a female Hedgehog.

- Don't be afraid to mix and match colors of felted wool. I used 2 shades and also the ribbed cuff part of the felted sweater, since I ran out of my first choice of brown mid-project. Even designers make mistakes!

BODY

1. Place 1 piece of the first body felted wool right side up on a flat surface and lay 1 piece of printed fabric face down on top, lining up the edges. Stitch them together by sewing either a backstitch by hand (page 23) or a straight stitch on a sewing machine (page 26), ¼″ (0.5cm) inside, along one edge. Repeat to join the other body pieces.

2. Lay the 2 joined pieces out flat, right sides together, lining up the stitched seams. Pin the Hedgehog body pattern on top (so the body area of the pattern covers the felted wool), lining up the join seamline on the pattern with the stitched seamline. Cut out the fabric pieces through both layers at once. Remove the pattern and construct the body (pages 13–14). Stuff it and add the pebble for weight. Add the card-stock base and attach the felted-wool base.

FACE

1. From craft felt, cut 2 eye circles and attach them using the mini buttons (page 8). Add the button nose.

2. For a female Hedgehog, cut the additional craft-felt square into a flower and attach it to the head using a button.

SPINES

1. Cut the remaining piece of felted wool into strips, about ⅝″ (just over 1.5cm) wide and then cut each strip into small rectangles about 1″ (2.5cm) long. Cut one end of each rectangle so it looks like the point of an arrow. None of the spines need to be exactly measured. Just do it by eye.

2. Attach the spines to the Hedgehog's body, one at a time, with 3 straight stitches (page 23) along the short straight edge opposite the arrow point using the pearl cotton 8. (figure A, page 45)

3. Keep randomly attaching the spines until the body is covered. You may need more or less, depending on how spiky you want your Hedgehog to be.

figure A

45

baby hedgehog

Finished size approximately 2″ x 4″ (5cm x 10cm)

You will need

- 2 pieces 3½″ × 3½″ (9cm × 9cm) of felted wool (page 8) for body

- 1 piece 2″ × 2½″ (5cm × 6.5cm) of felted wool (page 8) for base

- 1 piece 3″ × 7″ (7.5cm × 17.5cm) of felted wool (page 8) for spines

- 2 pieces 3½″ × 3½″ (9cm × 9cm) of printed fabric for body (face)

- 1 piece 1″ × 2″ (2.5cm × 5cm) of craft felt for eyes

- 2 mini buttons for eyes

- 1 button for nose

- 1 oval of card stock 1″ × 1½″ (2.5cm × 3.5cm) for base

- 1 pebble for weight

- Stuffing

- A selection of coordinating pearl cotton 8 threads for the appliqué and embroidery

- Sewing thread in a color to match the body parts, suitable for use either in a sewing machine or for hand stitching, for constructing the Baby Hedgehog

Additional for a female Baby Hedgehog:
- 2″ × 2″ (5cm × 5cm) square of craft felt and 1 button for flower

Read the Basic Instructions (pages 6–27) for more detailed information.

Patterns are on page 123. Trace and cut out the patterns.

BODY

1. Place 1 piece of the first body felted wool right side up on a flat surface and lay 1 piece of printed fabric face down on top, lining up the edges. Stitch them together by sewing either a backstitch by hand (page 23) or a straight stitch on a sewing machine (page 26) ¼″ (0.5cm) inside, along one edge. Repeat to join the other body pieces.

2. Lay the 2 joined pieces out flat, right sides together, lining up the stitched seams. Pin the Baby Hedgehog body pattern on top (so the body area of the pattern covers the felted wool), lining up the join seamline with the stitched seamline. Cut out the fabric pieces through both layers at once. Remove the pattern and construct the body (pages 13–14). Stuff it and add the pebble for weight. Add the card-stock base and attach the felted-wool base.

FACE

1. From craft felt, cut 2 eye circles and attach them using the mini buttons (page 8). Add the button nose.

2. For a female Hedgehog, cut the additional craft-felt square into a flower and attach it to the head using a button.

SPINES

1. Cut the remaining piece of felted wool into strips ½″ (1.5cm) wide. Then cut each strip into small rectangles 1″ (2.5cm) long. Cut 1 end of each rectangle so it looks like the point of an arrow. None of the spines need to be exactly measured; just do it by eye.

2. Attach the spines to the Baby Hedgehog's body one at a time with 3 straight stitches (page 23) along the short straight edge opposite the arrow point using the pearl cotton 8.

3. Keep randomly attaching the spines until the body is covered. You may need more or less, depending on how spiky you want your Baby Hedgehog to be.

robin

Finished size approximately 3½″ × 3½″ (9cm × 9cm)

Robins are cheeky, nosy little birds. One in particular, who lives in the hawthorn hedge in our back garden, spent a whole weekend last spring sitting and watching my husband build a new deck.

You will need

- 1 piece 6″ × 8″ (15cm × 20cm) of felted wool (page 8) for body and base
- 1 piece 3″ × 3″ (7.5cm × 7.5cm) of printed fabric for chest patch
- 1 piece 4″ × 4″ (10cm × 10cm) of printed fabric for wings
- 1 piece 4″ × 4″ (10cm × 10cm) of craft felt for beak and wings
- 1 piece 1″ × 2″ (2.5cm × 5cm) of craft felt for eyes
- 2 mini buttons for eyes

- 2 buttons to attach wings
- 1 oval of card stock 1″ × 1¼″ (2cm × 3cm) for base
- 1 pebble for weight
- Stuffing
- A selection of coordinating pearl cotton 8 threads for the appliqué and embroidery
- Sewing thread in a color to match the body parts, suitable for use either in a sewing machine or for hand stitching, for constructing the Robin

- As birds' feathers are often mottled in nature, there is a great opportunity here to use a printed felted wool; a stripy or fair isle pattern in soft hues of gray and brown will give a lovely muted effect.

- You could make more than one and use the Egg (page 107) pattern included with the Duck (page 102) to add to a family group.

- A Robin softie can make an excellent addition to your handmade nature table or Christmas table decoration.

Read the Basic Instructions (pages 6–27) for more detailed information.

Patterns are on page 124. Trace and cut out the patterns.

BODY

1. From the felted wool, cut 2 bodies (1 and 1 reverse) and 1 base.

2. Construct the body (pages 13–14). Stuff it and add the pebble for weight. Add the card-stock base and attach the felted-wool base.

3. From the first printed fabric, cut 1 chest patch and sew it in place, quite high up so it's also covering part of the face area (page 15).

EYES AND BEAK

1. From the craft felt, cut 2 eye circles and attach them using the mini buttons (page 8).

2. From the craft felt, cut a beak. Fold it in half and attach it to the Robin's face (pages 15–16), toward the top of the chest patch, using straight stitches (page 23).

WINGS

1. Cut 1 wing from the second printed fabric, flip the pattern, and then cut a second. Do the same again to cut 2 more wings from the craft felt. Pair up a craft-felt wing with a printed-fabric wing. With their wrong sides together, construct a wing (page 18) using the blanket stitch. Repeat for the other wing.

2. With a button, attach a wing, fabric side facing outward, to the side of the Robin. Repeat for the other wing.

robin ornament

The Robin theme continues with a miniature pattern—very quick to make in multiples and ideal as an addition to your Christmas tree.

Finished size approximately 2″ × 2½″ (5cm × 6.5cm), including the beak but not including the hanging thread

You will need

(Makes 1 Robin)

- 1 piece 1¼″ × 2″ (3cm × 5cm) of printed fabric for chest patch

- 1 piece 3″ × 5″ (7.5cm × 12.5cm) of craft felt for body

- 1 piece 1¼″ × 2″ (3cm × 5cm) of craft felt for beak and wing

- 1 piece 1″ × 1″ (2.5cm × 2.5cm) of craft felt for eye

- 1 mini button for eye

- Stuffing

- A selection of coordinating pearl cotton 8 threads for the appliqué and embroidery

- Sewing thread in a color to match the body parts, suitable for use either in a sewing machine or for hand stitching for constructing the Robin ornament

- 1 length 7″ (17.5cm) of thicker embroidery thread, pearl cotton 5, or wool yarn as a hanging thread

Read the Basic Instructions (pages 6–27) for more detailed information.

Patterns are on page 125. Trace and cut out the patterns.

BODY

1. From the craft felt, cut 2 bodies (1 and 1 reverse).

2. On the wrong side of 1 of the bodies, place the beak so it overlaps a little and sew it in place with the sewing thread. Fold the hanging thread in half and tie a knot at the cut ends. Place this at the top of the Robin's head, so the knot overlaps the felt body a little, and sew it in place just above the knot.

3. Place the second felt body piece on top of the first, wrong side down, so the stitching you have done is hidden.

4. Cut out a chest patch from the print fabric, place it in position on the top body piece, and pin. Stitch around the edge in a blanket stitch (page 22), using the pearl cotton 8, catching in the edge of the chest fabric as you go. Stop when there is a ¾˝ (2cm) gap, push in a little stuffing with the stuffer stick (page 7), and continue with the blanket stitch to close up.

5. Add a few random straight stitches (page 23) around the curved side of the chest patch. Cut an eye circle and sew on the mini button with the circle of felt beneath.

6. Finally, from the craft felt, cut the wing and attach it with a few random straight stitches.

tip

Vary the direction of the patterns when making multiple Robin ornaments so some will be facing to the right and some to the left.

bumblebee

Finished size approximately 2½″ × 3″ (6.5cm × 7.5cm)

Bizzy, buzzy, fuzzy little bumblebees always work well in crafts. And the best thing about these bees is they have no sting—unless you accidentally leave a pin in!

You will need

- 1 piece 4″ × 6″ (10cm × 15cm) of felted wool (page 8) for body and base
- 1 piece 2″ × 3″ (5cm × 7.5cm) of printed fabric for stripes
- 1 piece 2″ × 4″ (5cm × 10cm) of craft felt for wings
- 1 piece 1″ × 2″ (2.5cm × 5cm) of craft felt for eyes
- 2 mini buttons for eyes
- 1 oval of card stock ¾″ × 1″ (2cm × 2.5cm) for base

- 1 small pebble for weight
- Stuffing
- A selection of coordinating pearl cotton 8 threads for the appliqué and embroidery
- Sewing thread in a color to match the body parts, suitable for use either in a sewing machine or for hand stitching, for constructing the Bumblebee
- Black pearl cotton 5 for antennae
- 1 length 7″ (17.5cm) of thicker embroidery thread, pearl cotton 5, or wool yarn as a hanging thread (optional)

countryside **softies**

Read the Basic Instructions (pages 6–27) for more detailed information.

Patterns are on page 125. Trace and cut out the patterns.

BODY

1. From the felted wool, cut 2 bodies (1 and 1 reverse) and 1 base. From the craft felt, cut 2 wings.

2. Place 1 body right side up on a flat surface, lay the 2 wings on top as illustrated, and finish off with the other body on top, this time right side down.

3. Construct the body (pages 13–14). Stuff it and add the pebble for weight. Add the card-stock base and attach the felted-wool base. Since this is such a small project, the card-stock base may need to be trimmed if it's too big.

tip

Adding the pebble weight and the card-stock base makes the Bee able to stand on a flat surface. If you want to hang your Bumblebee up, instead leave them both out and close up the Bumblebee's body using a whipstitch (page 26) in a sewing thread that matches the body color. Remember to add the hanging thread (see Robin Ornament, page 52).

STRIPES

1. From printed fabric, cut 2 stripes (1 and 1 reverse from each stripe pattern).

2. Holding the Bee with the wings on the left, pin on the first 2 stripes side by side at an angle, so they are not quite horizontal. Stitch them in place with random straight stitches (page 23), using the pearl cotton 8. Repeat on the other side of the Bumblebee.

EYES AND ANTENNAE

1. From craft felt, cut 2 eye circles. Again holding the Bumblebee with the wings to the left, add the eyes by sewing on the 2 mini buttons, side by side, with a circle of craft felt underneath each one.

2. Using the pearl cotton 5, add 2 antennae (page 20).

butterfly

Finished size approximately 2½″ × 3¼″ (6.5cm × 8cm)

Butterfly, flutterbye—who didn't enjoy chasing butterflies as a child?

You will need

- 1 piece 2″ × 2½″ (5cm × 6.5cm) of felted wool (page 8) for body

- 2 pieces, each 3″ × 4″ (7.5cm × 10cm), of different printed fabrics for wings

- 2 mini buttons for eyes

- 1 piece 3″ × 4″ (7.5cm × 10cm) of interfacing (page 8) for wings

- Stuffing

- A selection of coordinating pearl cotton 8 threads for embroidery and hanging thread

- Sewing thread in a color to match the body parts, suitable for use either in a sewing machine or for hand stitching, for constructing the Butterfly

- Brown pearl cotton 5 for the antennae

Read the Basic Instructions (pages 6–27) for more detailed information.

Patterns are on page 125. Trace and cut out the patterns.

BODY

1. From felted wool, cut 2 bodies.

2. Construct the body (pages 13–14). Since the Butterfly is so small, sew as close to the edge as you can. Stuff the body and whipstitch (page 26) it closed.

WINGS

1. From 1 of the printed fabrics, cut 2 wings (1 and 1 reverse). Repeat with the other printed fabric to make the underneath layer and also cut 2 wings from the interfacing. Place each wing in a pile, with a printed fabric at the top and bottom, wrong sides together, with the interfacing sandwiched in between.

2. Sew all the way around, just less than ¼˝ (0.5cm) in from the edge of each wing, either by hand using a running stitch (page 24)

in pearl cotton 8 or on a sewing machine using a straight stitch (page 26).

3. From the 2 wings, choose which fabric you want facing the top and attach 1 wing to the side of the Butterfly, using random straight stitches (page 23) in pearl cotton 8. Repeat for the other wing.

ANTENNAE AND EYES

1. Using the pearl cotton 5, add 2 antennae (page 20).

2. Add the 2 button eyes (page 17).

3. Finish by adding an extra length of thread—pearl cotton 8 will do—as a hanging thread. Anchor it to the Butterfly, centering it on the body between the wings so it hangs straight when held in the air. Decide how long you want the hanger to be and then fold over the other end of the thread and tie a knot to make a loop.

tips

- Because the Butterfly wings are small and fiddly, it is easier to sew the layers together on a sewing machine than by hand.

- Make your Butterfly into a brooch by attaching a brooch pin to the underside of the body.

making a mobile

A simple way of using all three of the insect patterns—Bumblebee (page 54), Butterfly (page 58), and Dragonfly (page 114)—is to display them as a mobile.

You will need

- Selection of insect softies (page 54, page 58, and page 114)
- Pearl cotton 5 a little longer than the total length you want your mobile to be

MOBILE

1. Thread a needle with a long length of pearl cotton 5 and tie a knot at the other end. Starting with the lowest softie in the mobile, pass the needle up through its body and out through the top. Pull gently until the knot rests against the bottom of the softie.

2. Decide how far apart you want your softies to be. Then leave a suitable gap in the thread and tie a knot where you want the next softie to sit. Again, pass the needle up through the body of the next softie and out through the top. Pull gently so the second knot in the thread rests against the softie to hold it in place.

3. Repeat for each softie you want to add. Once you are finished, leave a length of thread free above the final softie to make a hanging loop. Decide how long you want the hanger to be, fold over the end of the thread, and tie a knot to make a loop at the top for hanging.

amongst the woodlands

squirrel

Finished size approximately 6″ × 7″ (15cm × 17.5cm)

When I was a child, my family lived in Formby in the United Kingdom. One of the special things about this village is that it sits right on the coast and is home to one of only five remaining red squirrel sanctuaries. Of course, one thing about the squirrel sanctuary is that although it is mostly fenced, the squirrels can climb and quite often wander off into the village. It was hard to remember these little amber-colored creatures are an endangered species when they were so often hanging out in the back garden.

You will need

- 1 piece 8″ × 12″ (20cm × 30cm) of felted wool (page 8) for body, base, and feet

- 1 piece 4″ × 5″ (10cm × 12.5cm) of felted wool (page 8) for feet and ears

- 3 pieces 2½″ × 9¼″ (6.5cm × 24cm) of felted wool (page 8) for tail

- 1 piece 1″ × 2″ (2.5cm × 5cm) of felted wool (page 8) or craft felt for eyes

- 1 piece 4″ × 4″ (10cm × 10cm) of printed fabric for chest and ears

- 2 mini buttons for eyes

- 1 button for nose

- 1 length 9¾″ (24cm) of garden wire (page 10) for tail

- 1 oval of card stock 1¼″ × 1½″ (3cm × 4cm) for base

- 1 pebble for weight

- Stuffing

- A selection of coordinating pearl cotton 8 threads for the appliqué and embroidery

- Sewing thread in a color to match the body parts, suitable for use either in a sewing machine or for hand stitching, for constructing the Squirrel

Read the Basic Instructions (pages 6–27) for more detailed information.

Patterns are on page 126. Trace and cut out the patterns.

BODY

1. From the felted wool, cut 2 bodies (1 and 1 reverse), 1 base, and 2 feet.

2. Set aside the feet for now. Construct the body (pages 13–14). Stuff it and add the pebble for weight. Add the card-stock base and attach the felted-wool base.

3. From the printed fabric, cut 1 chest patch and sew it in place (page 15).

FACE AND EARS

1. From the second felted wool and the printed fabric, cut 4 ears (2 from each fabric). Place a felted wool and a fabric ear wrong sides together and sew around the curved edges in a blanket stitch (page 22), leaving the bottom edge unstitched. Fold the bottom sides of the ear into the center, printed-fabric side inward, and sew it in place. Repeat for the second ear.

2. From the felted wool or craft felt, cut 2 eye circles. Position 1 on the side of the Squirrel's head and anchor it in place by sewing a mini button in the center (page 17). Repeat on the other side of the head for the other eye.

3. Stitch on the remaining button for the nose and add a mouth (page 17).

FEET

From the second piece of felted wool, cut 2 more feet and sort the feet into pairs with the first felted-wool feet pieces. Pin each set, wrong sides together. Construct the feet (page 18) using a blanket stitch. Add 2 or 3 vertical backstitch lines, about ¾˝ (2cm) long, to create toes. Repeat for the other foot and attach both feet in place on the body.

TAIL

1. Place 1 of the tail pieces of felted wool on top of another piece. Then lay the length of garden wire down the center (it doesn't have to be exact) and place the remaining piece of felted wool on top. Pin to hold it roughly in place.

2. Stitch the tail using one of the following methods:

Method One

By hand: Using matching thread, sew down both sides of the garden wire, stitching through all 3 layers of felted wool in a running stitch (page 24), to trap the wire between the layers.

Method Two

By sewing machine: Set the machine to zigzag stitch, stitch length of 2mm and a maximum width setting, usually classed as a 5mm. Place all 3 layers under the machine foot so the needle is going to come down on one side of the garden wire and then zigzag over the wire to the other side. Slowly stitch, using matching thread, to trap the wire between the layers.

3. Add a few stitches at one of the open ends to stop it from poking out. Then cut a ½˝ (1cm) fringe on each side of the tail, stopping just short of the central stitching.

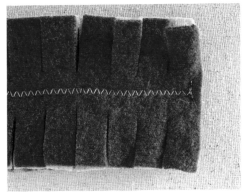

Stitch to encase the wire; the stitching here is done in white to make it visible.

4. From the other—still open—end of the garden wire, push back the felted wool a little so the tail gathers and exposes about 2″ (5cm) of the wire. Keeping hold of the wire, begin to twist the felted wool so it spins around the wire, making the fringe spread out. Then bend the felted-wool tail end of the wire into an "S" shape to hold the fringing in place. Bend the exposed wire into a U-shaped hook.

5. Poke the hook into the Squirrel softie's bottom (ouch!), bringing it back out ¼˝ (0.5cm) away through the felted wool. Bend the final end of the wire around and push it against the Squirrel's body. Hold all this in place with a few stitches at the base and then move up the tail, anchoring it to the Squirrel as it follows the curve of the Squirrel's back to hold it all in place.

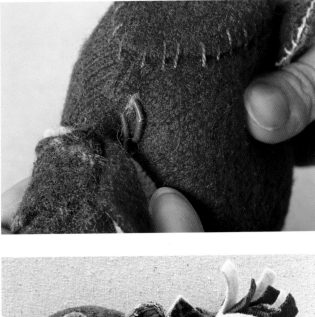

chestnut

Finished size approximately 1½" × 1¾" (3.5cm × 4cm)

Collecting chestnuts from buckeye or horse chestnut trees is a childhood tradition, the aim always being to see who could knock down the largest shell in the hope it would contain a winning chestnut.

You will need

- 1 piece 4″ × 4″ (10cm × 10cm) of felted wool (page 8) for Chestnut

- 1 piece 2″ × 2″ (5cm × 5cm) of felted wool for Chestnut top

- 1 pebble for weight

- Stuffing

- A selection of coordinating pearl cotton 8 threads for the appliqué and embroidery

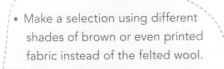

- Make a selection using different shades of brown or even printed fabric instead of the felted wool.

- The Chestnut sizes will vary depending on the size of pebble and how much stuffing you add.

Read the Basic Instructions (pages 6–27) for more detailed information.

Patterns are on page 138. Trace and cut out the patterns.

CHESTNUT

1. From the first piece of felted wool, cut the Chestnut.

2. Thread a needle with some pearl cotton 8 and knot the other end. Sew a running stitch (page 24) all the way around the outside, roughly ¼˝ (0.5cm) in from the edge.

3. Pull the thread to gather it slightly and place a little bit of stuffing in the center, followed by the pebble, also wrapped in stuffing. Keep pulling the thread to gather the fabric tighter, adding more stuffing just before you close it up if need be. Once you are happy with the shape, add a few stitches to secure the gathered fabric in place.

4. Cut the oval top from the other piece of felted wool, place it over the gathered end of the Chestnut, and sew it in place with a few random straight stitches (page 23).

5. Add a central area to the Chestnut by sewing 4 straight stitches on top of each other to form a star.

tip

Use some extra pearl cotton 8 and add a hanging thread to display the Chestnut. Attach the thread to the center and decide how long you want the hanger to be. Fold over the other end of the thread and tie a knot to make a loop.

badger

Finished size approximately 6″ × 9″ (15cm × 22.5cm), including the snout and tail

It was a particular fabric that brought the idea of a badger to mind. I was caught short one day for something printed in blacks and grays, so I paid a visit to my local thrift store. Immediately, a shirt jumped out from the rack as being ideal, and the fabric has been used many times and has become many different softies.

You will need

- 1 piece 8″ × 14″ (20cm × 35cm) of felted wool (page 8) for body

- 1 piece 6″ × 8″ (15cm × 20cm) of felted wool (page 8) for base, feet, ears, and tail

- 1 piece 1″ × 2″ (2.5cm × 5cm) of felted wool (page 8) or craft felt for eyes

- 1 piece 6″ × 10″ (15cm × 25cm) of printed fabric for chest/face appliqué

- 1 piece 5″ × 5″ (12.5cm × 12.5cm) of printed fabric for ears and tail

- 2 mini buttons for eyes

- 2 buttons for nose and attaching tail

- 1 oval of card stock 1¼″ × 2¼″ (3cm × 5.5cm) for base

- 1 pebble for weight

- Stuffing

- A selection of coordinating pearl cotton 8 threads for the appliqué and embroidery

- Sewing thread in a color to match the body parts, suitable for use either in a sewing machine or for hand stitching, for constructing the Badger

Read the Basic Instructions (pages 6–27) for more detailed information.

Patterns are on pages 127–128. Trace and cut out the patterns.

BODY

1. From the first felted wool, cut 2 bodies (1 and 1 reverse). From the second felted wool, cut a base.

2. Construct the body (pages 13–14). Stuff it and add the pebble for weight. Add the card-stock base and attach the felted-wool base.

3. From the printed fabric, cut 2 chest/face patches (1 and 1 reverse).

4. Pin the 2 chest/face patches right sides together and stitch down the straight edge marked "join" on the pattern, either by hand in a backstitch (page 23) or with a straight stitch on a sewing machine (page 26), ¼" (0.5cm) in from the edge. Open the fabric and pin it in place on the Badger's body, lining up the fabric seam with the seam on the body. Attach it with random straight stitches (page 23). You can also add some decorative embroidery stitches to the chest area. I've added some straight-stitch crosses and seed stitch (pages 23 and 25).

HEAD AND FEET

1. From felted wool or craft felt, cut 2 eye circles and attach them using the mini buttons (page 8).

2. Stitch 1 of the buttons to the end of the snout as a nose.

3. From the second felted wool and the printed fabric, cut 4 ears (2 from each fabric).

4. Use a blanket stitch (page 22) to construct the ears (page 17), using a felted-wool piece and a printed-fabric piece, and attach them to the head.

5. Cut 4 feet shapes from the second felted wool.

6. Construct the feet (page 18) in pairs with wrong side together, using a blanket stitch. Add 4 or 5 vertical backstitch lines, ¾″ (2cm) long, to create toes. Attach both feet side by side to the front of the Badger's body.

TAIL

1. Cut 1 tail from the second felted wool, flip the pattern, and cut 1 from the second printed fabric.

2. Construct the tail (page 19) using a blanket stitch. Add some horizontal straight stitches, just stitching through the fabric layer, to emulate the direction of the fur to the end of the tail.

3. Attach the tail to the rear of the body, fabric side facing forward, using the remaining button.

owl

Finished size approximately 4″ × 6½″ (10cm × 16.5cm)

The very first drawing I have a memory of doing at school was of an owl. It sat perched on a branch. The first softie I designed once I'd found my "style" was also an owl—fate I guess!

You will need

- 1 piece 8″ × 10″ (20cm × 25cm) of felted wool (page 8) for body and base

- 1 piece 4″ × 5″ (10cm × 12.5cm) of felted wool (page 8) for face

- 1 piece 5″ × 6″ (12.5cm × 15cm) of felted wool (page 8) for wings

- 1 piece 5″ × 5″ (12.5cm × 12.5cm) of felted wool (page 8) for claws

- 1 piece 2″ × 3″ (5cm × 7.5cm) of craft felt for eyes

- 1 piece 1½″ × 3″ (4cm × 7.5cm) of craft felt for beak

- 1 piece 4″ × 5″ (10cm × 12.5cm) of printed fabric for tummy patch and crest

- 1 piece 5″ × 6″ (12.5cm × 15cm) of printed fabric for wings

- 2 mini buttons for eyes

- 2 buttons to attach wings

- 1 oval of card stock 1¼″ × 1½″ (3cm × 4cm) for base

- 1 pebble for weight

- Stuffing

- A selection of coordinating pearl cotton 8 threads for the appliqué and embroidery

- Sewing thread in a color to match the body parts, suitable for use either in a sewing machine or for hand stitching, for constructing the Owl

Read the Basic Instructions (pages 6–27) for more detailed information.

Patterns are on page 129. Trace and cut out the patterns.

BODY

1. From the first felted wool, cut 2 bodies and a base shape.

2. Construct the body (pages 13–14). Stuff it and add the pebble for weight. Add the card-stock base and attach the felted-wool base.

3. From the first printed fabric, cut a tummy patch and a crest.

4. Attach the tummy patch and the crest with random straight stitches (page 15). You can also add some decorative embroidery stitches to the tummy area. I've added fly stitches to look like feathers (page 25).

FACE, EYES, AND BEAK

1. From the second felted wool, cut a face, and from the first craft felt, cut 2 eyes.

2. Pin all 3 of these shapes in place on the body. Secure the face and eye patches with random straight stitches (page 23) around the edges of the eyes, catching the eye patch, face, and Owl body in each stitch. Add a mini button in the center to finish the eyes.

3. From the second craft felt, cut a beak. Fold the beak in half and attach it (pages 15–16) between the Owl's eyes using 3 straight stitches (page 23).

WINGS

1. From the second printed fabric and the third felted wool, cut 4 wings (1 and 1 reverse from each fabric).

2. Pair up a felted-wool piece with a printed-fabric piece, wrong sides together. Construct a wing (page 18) using a blanket stitch. Attach the wing to the side of the Owl using a button, with the fabric side facing outward and with the longest feather toward the back. Repeat for the other wing.

CLAWS

1. From the remaining felted wool, cut 4 claw shapes.

2. Pair up 2 shapes with wrong sides together and construct the claws (page 18) using a blanket stitch. Attach the claws in place, side by side, to the front of the Owl's body.

baby owl

Finished size approximately 3½″ × 3½″ (9cm × 9cm)

You will need

- 1 piece 6″ × 8″ (15cm × 20cm) of felted wool (page 8) for body and base

- 1 piece 3″ × 3½″ (7.5cm × 9cm) of felted wool (page 8) for face

- 1 piece 3″ × 4″ (7.5cm × 10cm) of felted wool (page 8) for wings

- 1 piece 1½″ × 3″ (3.5cm × 7.5cm) of craft felt for eyes and optional heart

- 1 piece 1″ × 2″ (2.5cm × 5cm) of craft felt for beak

- 1 piece 3″ × 3½″ (7.5cm × 9cm) of printed fabric for tummy patch and crest

- 1 piece 3″ × 4″ (7.5cm × 10cm) of printed fabric for wings

- 2 mini buttons for eyes

- 2 buttons to attach wings

- 1 heart-shaped button (optional)

- 1 oval of card stock 1½″ × 2″ (3.5cm × 5cm) for base

- 1 pebble for weight

- Stuffing

- A selection of coordinating pearl cotton 8 threads for the appliqué and embroidery

- Sewing thread in a color to match the body parts, suitable for use either in a sewing machine or for hand stitching, for constructing the Baby Owl

countryside **softies**

Read the Basic Instructions (pages 6–27) for more detailed information.

Patterns are on page 130. Trace and cut out the patterns.

BODY

1. From the first felted wool, cut 2 bodies and a base shape.

2. Construct the body (pages 13–14). Stuff it and add the pebble for weight. Add the card-stock base and attach the felted-wool base.

3. From the first printed fabric, cut a tummy patch and a crest.

4. Attach the tummy patch and the crest (page 15) with random straight stitches (page 23).

FACE, EYES, AND BEAK

1. From the second felted wool, cut a face, and from the first craft felt, cut 2 eyes.

2. Pin all 3 of these shapes in place on the body. Secure the face and eye patches with random straight stitches around the edges of the eyes, catching the eye patch, face, and Owl body in each stitch. Add a mini button in the center to finish the eyes.

3. Cut a beak from the second craft felt. Fold it in half and attach it (pages 15–16) between the Baby Owl's eyes, using 3 straight stitches (page 23).

WINGS

1. From the second printed fabric and the third felted wool, cut 4 wings (1 and 1 reverse from each fabric).

2. Pair up a felted-wool piece with a printed-fabric piece, wrong sides together. Construct a wing (page 18) using a blanket stitch. Attach the wing to the side of the Owl using a button, with the fabric side facing outward and with the longest feather toward the back. Repeat for the other wing.

tips

- Add a decoration to your Baby Owl; I've added a heart-shaped button over a piece of heart-shaped craft felt.

- You could also add a flower to make a female Owl. Refer to either the Rabbits (page 34), the Hedgehogs (page 42), or the Mice (page 82) for instructions.

- Add an Egg to your Owls, using the pattern included with the Duck (page 107).

mouse

Finished size, including the tail, approximately 4″ × 4″ (10cm × 10cm)

There used to be a television series called *Bagpuss* in the United Kingdom. The mice were ornamental carvings on the wooden mouse organ. They came to life and mended the broken objects brought into the shop where they lived. While they were mending, the mice all sang an appropriate song:

We will fix it, we will stitch it, we will make it like new, new, new…

So you can understand my association of mice with handicrafts.

You will need
(Makes 1 adult male or female)

- 1 piece 6″ × 9″ (15cm × 22.5cm) of felted wool (page 8) for body, base, ears, and tail

- 1 piece 1″ × 2″ (2.5cm × 5cm) of craft felt for eyes

- 1 piece 2″ × 2″ (5cm × 5cm) of craft felt for heart personalization patch

- 1 piece 6″ × 6″ (15cm × 15cm) of printed fabric for tummy patch, ears, and tail

- 3 mini buttons for eyes and nose

- 1 button for tail

- 1 circle of card stock 1¼″ × 1¼″ (3cm × 3cm) for the base

- 1 pebble for weight

- Stuffing

- White pearl cotton 5 for the whiskers

- A selection of coordinating pearl cotton 8 threads for the appliqué and embroidery

- Sewing thread in a color to match the body parts, suitable for use either in a sewing machine or for hand stitching, for constructing the Mouse

Additional for a female Mouse:
- 1 piece 1½″ × 1½″ (3.5cm × 3.5cm) of craft felt and 1 button for flower

Additional for a male Mouse:
- 1 piece 1″ × 1½″ (2.5cm × 3.5cm) of craft felt for bow tie

Read the Basic Instructions (pages 6–27) for more detailed information.

Patterns are on page 131. Trace and cut out the patterns.

BODY

1. From the felted wool, cut 2 bodies (1 and 1 reverse), 1 base, 2 ears, and 1 tail.

2. Construct the body (pages 13–14). Stuff it and add the pebble for weight. Add the card-stock base and attach the felted-wool base.

3. From the printed fabric, cut 1 tummy patch. Attach it with random straight stitches (page 23).

FACE

From the craft felt, cut 2 eye circles and attach them using the mini buttons (page 8). Also attach the button nose and add the whiskers (page 20).

EARS, TAIL, AND OTHER DECORATION

1. From the printed fabric, cut 2 more ears.

2. Construct the ears using a felted-wool piece and a printed-fabric piece (page 17), wrong sides together, using a blanket stitch. Attach them to the head using straight stitches.

3. From the printed fabric, cut a tail (1 reverse).

4. Construct the tail (page 19) using a felted-wool piece and a printed-fabric piece, wrong sides together, using a blanket stitch (page 22).

5. Attach the tail, fabric side facing forward, to the rear of the body, using the remaining button.

tip

Make an individual Mouse as a birthday gift or Valentine's Day gift for a loved one, or make a whole family.

6. For a female Mouse, cut the additional craft-felt square into a flower and attach it to the head using a button. For a male Mouse, cut the additional craft-felt rectangle into a bow tie and attach it to the front of the neck with 2 crossed straight stitches, using pearl cotton 8.

PERSONALIZATION PATCH

1. Cut a heart from the square of craft felt. To personalize it, mark the lettering if need be, using your own handwriting, and then begin embroidering either in a backstitch (page 23) using the pearl cotton 8 or via free-motion machine stitching (page 27). If you're using free-motion embroidery, place a heart shape of interfacing underneath the felt to strengthen it.

2. Trim off any excess interfacing.

3. Attach the heart to the Mouse's back, on the other side from the tail, using random straight stitches (page 23).

baby mouse

Finished size approximately 2½˝ × 4˝ (6.5cm × 10cm)

You will need

(Makes 1 Baby Mouse)

- 1 piece 6˝ × 8˝ (15cm × 20cm) of felted wool (page 8) for body, base, and ears

- 1 piece 1˝ × 2˝ (2.5cm × 5cm) of craft felt for eyes

- 1 piece 2˝ × 2˝ (5cm × 5cm) of craft felt for personalization patch

- 1 piece 3˝ × 4˝ (7.5cm × 10cm) of printed fabric for tummy patch and ears

- 3 mini buttons for eyes and nose

- 1 oval of card stock ¾˝ × 1˝ (2cm × 2.5cm) for base

- 1 pebble for weight

- Stuffing

- White pearl cotton 5 for the whiskers

- A selection of coordinating pearl cotton 8 threads for the appliqué and embroidery

- Sewing thread in a color to match the body parts, suitable for use either in a sewing machine or for hand stitching, for constructing the Baby Mouse

- 1 length 5˝ (12.5cm) of wool yarn for the tail

Additional for a female Mouse:
- 1 piece 1½˝ × 1½˝ (3.5cm × 3.5cm) of craft felt and 1 button for flower

Additional for a male Mouse:
- 1 piece 1˝ × 1½˝ (2.5cm × 3.5cm) of craft felt for bow tie

Read the Basic Instructions (pages 6–27) for more detailed information.

Patterns are on page 132. Trace and cut out the patterns.

BODY

1. From the felted wool, cut 2 bodies (1 and 1 reverse), 1 base, and 2 ears.

2. Construct the body (pages 13–14). Stuff it and add the pebble for weight. Add the card-stock base and attach the felted-wool base.

3. From the printed fabric, cut out a tummy patch and attach it using random straight stitches (page 23).

FACE

1. From the craft felt, cut 2 eye circles (page 17) and position 1 on the side of the Baby Mouse's head. Anchor it in place by sewing a mini button in the center. Repeat on the other side of the head for the other eye.

2. Stitch the remaining mini button on as a nose and add the whiskers (page 20).

EARS, TAIL, AND OTHER DECORATION

1. From the printed fabric, cut 2 ear shapes. Pair up a felted-wool and a printed-fabric ear, wrong sides together (page 17), and sew a blanket stitch around the edge, leaving the bottom edge unstitched. Repeat for the other ear. Attach both ears in place using straight stitches.

2. For the tail, thread a needle with the wool yarn and tie a knot in one end. Poke the needle in between the fabric tummy patch and the Baby Mouse's body. Near the center, begin pushing the needle point into the softie so it comes out the other side in the position you want the tail to start. Pull the yarn all the way through. The knot to secure it is now hidden underneath the tummy patch. Unthread the needle and trim the wool yarn to the desired tail length. Tie a knot toward the end to prevent the yarn from unraveling. (See photo below).

3. For a female Mouse, cut the additional craft-felt square into a flower and attach it to the head using a button. For a male Mouse, cut the additional craft-felt rectangle into a tie and attach to the front of the neck with 2 crossed straight stitches, using pearl cotton 8.

PERSONALIZATION PATCH

1. From the second craft felt, cut a heart. Follow the instructions in Personalization Patch (page 85).

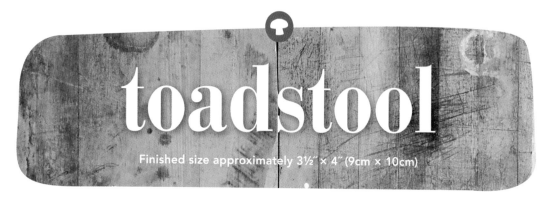

toadstool

Finished size approximately 3½″ × 4″ (9cm × 10cm)

About a year or so after I began craft blogging, I posted a tutorial for making a little Toadstool. The Toadstool proved very popular, and the project evolved into my very first international craft swap. Pretty soon almost 70 crafters from around the globe had joined, many adding their own ideas to their Toadstool. This project is a variation on the same idea.

You will need

- 1 piece 4½″ × 5″ (11cm × 12.5cm) of felted wool (page 8) for Toadstool cap

- 1 piece 3″ × 3″ (7.5cm × 7.5cm) of felted wool (page 8) for base

- 1 piece 6″ × 8″ (15cm × 20cm) of printed fabric for stalk, underside of cap, and top patch

- Selection of buttons for the spots

- 1 circle of card stock 1¼″ × 1¼″ (3cm × 3cm) for base

- 1 pebble for weight

- Stuffing

- A selection of coordinating pearl cotton 8 threads for the appliqué and embroidery

- Sewing thread in a color to match the felted wool and fabrics, suitable for use either in a sewing machine or for hand stitching, for constructing the Toadstool

Read the Basic Instructions (pages 6–27) for more detailed information.

Patterns are on page 132. Trace and cut out the patterns.

STALK

1. From the printed fabric, cut 2 stalks.

2. Place the stalk pieces right sides together and pin. Stitch both sides just less than ¼″ (0.5cm) in from the edge, leaving the top and the bottom open. Turn the tube right side out.

3. Place a small ball of stuffing inside the tube, at the bottom of the stalk, to hold it open while attaching the base. Lay the card stock over the stuffing, place the circle of felted wool on top, and sew it in place with random straight stitches. Turn under the bottom edge of the stalk a little bit as you stitch.

4. Stand the stalk base on a flat surface, tuck the wrapped pebble into the bottom of the stalk to weight the Toadstool, and continue to fill it with stuffing.

TOADSTOOL CAP

1. From both the felted wool and the printed fabric, cut a cap (2 total). Fold the printed-fabric piece in half, and then in half again into quadrants. Make a small cut in the center. Open the cap up flat, and using the hole as a starting point, cut a small circle from the center, no larger than ¾″ (2cm) across.

2. Place both the cap pieces wrong sides together and stitch a blanket stitch all the way around the edge to join them. Stuff the cap through the printed-fabric hole, leaving a well in the center for the stalk.

3. Take a small amount of stuffing, flatten it a little in your hands, and cut it into a rough circle 2″ (5cm) across. Cut a hole in the center of this, large enough for the stalk to go through.

4. Turn the cap upside down, lay the stuffing circle on top, lining up the central holes, and push the open end of the stalk into position through the stuffing "doughnut" and against the cap.

5. Stitch the stalk in place on the cap with large random straight stitches (page 23).

SPOTS

1. Cut the spot patch from the printed fabric and attach it to the cap with random straight stitches.

2. Add a selection of buttons in various sizes and colors to decorate the cap.

tips

- Make multiple Toadstools and build your own handcrafted terrarium by placing them inside the base of a glass jar filled with pebbles.

- Display along with the Chestnut (page 70) for a softie nature table.

along the riverbank

otter

Finished size approximately 3½˝ × 6˝ (9cm × 15cm)

As a child, I remember watching the film *Ring of Bright Water* and thinking it was an enchanting film (albeit a little sad in places). Set on the west coast of Scotland, it is a charming tale centered around the real star of the story, Mij the Otter.

You will need

- 1 piece 12˝ × 12˝ (30cm × 30cm) of felted wool (page 8) for body, base, ears, snout, arms, feet, and tail

- 1 piece 1˝ × 2˝ (2.5cm × 5cm) of craft felt for eyes

- 1 piece 4˝ × 5˝ (10cm × 12.5cm) of printed fabric for chest patch and snout

- 1 piece 6˝ × 8˝ (15cm × 20cm) of printed fabric for ears, arms, feet, and tail

- 2 mini buttons for eyes

- 1 button for nose

- 2 buttons to attach arms

- 1 oval of card stock 1˝ × 1½˝ (2.5cm × 3cm) for base

- 1 pebble for weight

- Stuffing

- A selection of coordinating pearl cotton 8 threads for the appliqué and embroidery

- Sewing thread in a color to match the body parts, suitable for use either in a sewing machine or for hand stitching, for constructing the Otter

Additional for Fish:

- 1 piece 4˝ × 4˝ (10cm × 10cm) of craft felt for body

- A selection of coordinating pearl cotton 8 threads for the embroidery

- 1 mini button for the eye

tip

The Fish can be pretty much any color—blue, orange, gray—it's up to you.

Read the Basic Instructions (pages 6–27) for more detailed information.

Patterns are on pages 133–134. Trace and cut out the patterns.

BODY

1. From the felted wool, cut 2 bodies, 1 base, 2 ears, 2 arms, 2 feet, 1 snout, and 1 tail.

2. Construct the body (pages 13–14). Stuff it and add the pebble for weight. Add the card-stock base and attach the felted-wool base.

3. From the first printed fabric, cut 1 chest patch.

4. Sew the chest patch in place (page 15) using random straight stitches, making sure the top of the chest patch lines up with the marked line on the pattern roughly halfway up the head.

SNOUT, EARS, AND EYES

1. From the first printed fabric, cut a snout.

2. Construct the snout using a felted-wool piece and a printed-fabric piece (pages 15–16). Attach it to the face using random straight stitches, with the printed fabric on the underside, slightly overlapping the top of the chest patch. Add the button nose.

3. From the second printed fabric, cut 2 ears.

4. Construct the ears from a felted-wool piece and a printed-fabric piece (page 17) using a blanket stitch (page 22). leaving the bottom edge unstitched. Fold the ear in half vertically, printed-fabric side inward, and sew it in place.

5. From craft felt, cut 2 eye circles and attach them using the mini buttons (page 8).

TAIL, ARMS, AND FEET

1. From the second printed fabric, cut a tail.

2. Construct the tail using a felted-wool piece and a printed-fabric piece. With right sides together, stitch a ¼″ (0.5cm) seam allowance all around, except leave the top (the wider end) open. Turn the tail right side out and stuff it, using the stuffer stick to get the stuffing all the way down to the end. Don't overstuff the tail, as it will need to bend. Attach the tail to the rear of the Otter using random straight stitches. Curl the tail around the body toward the front. Attach the tail in position using the method in Making Feet/Claws and Arms (page 18).

3. From the second printed fabric, cut 2 arms. Construct the arms from a felted-wool piece and a printed-fabric piece (page 18) using the blanket stitch, but before finishing, leave a small gap and add a little stuffing. Continue with the blanket stitch to close up the gap.

4. Add 2 or 3 straight stitches to the narrower end (or paw end) on the felted-wool side to make fingers.

5. Attach the arm to the right side of the Otter, about 1˝ (2.5cm) below the snout, printed-fabric side facing inward, using 1 of the buttons. (See photo, page 19.) Repeat for the other arm, except attach this arm on the left side with the remaining button. Put it a little higher up than the first arm. (See photo, page 95.)

6. From the second piece of printed fabric, cut 2 feet. Construct the feet (page 18), using a felted-wool piece and a printed-fabric piece, wrong sides together, using a blanket stitch and leaving the bottom straight edge open. Stuff and close up the gap.

7. Add 2 or 3 backstitch lines, ½˝ (1cm) long, to create toes.

8. Attach the feet in place with the printed fabric on the inside.

fish

1. From the craft felt, cut 2 Fish and place them wrong sides together.

2. Construct the Fish using the blanket stitch (page 22), but before finishing, leave a small gap and add a little stuffing. Continue with the blanket stitch to close the gap.

3. Holding the Fish with the tail to the right, add a few horizontal straight stitches (page 23) to decorate the tail and a few random fly stitches (page 25) to the body to imitate scales. Add the button eye.

4. With the Otter facing you and the Fish pointing downward to the left at 45°, place the left paw so it overlaps the top of the Fish's body slightly and anchor it in place with a few stitches (see Making Feet/Claws and Arms, page 18). Similarly, place the Otter's other paw on the bottom edge of the Fish's tail and stitch it in place.

swan

Finished size approximately 5″ × 6″ (12.5cm × 15cm)

Swans are considered to be majestic, graceful birds.
While calm and serene on the surface, underwater their
legs are paddling as fast as they can. In human life, this is
a skill many adults often seek to emulate.

You will need

- 1 piece 6″ × 12″ (15cm × 30cm) of felted wool (page 8) for body

- 1 piece 2″ × 3″ (5cm × 7.5cm) of felted wool (page 8) for top of beak

- 1 piece 2″ × 3″ (5cm × 7.5cm) of felted wool (page 8) for bottom of beak

- 1 piece 5″ × 8″ (12.5cm × 20cm) of printed fabric for chest and base patch and wing decorations behind buttons

- 1 piece 6″ × 8″ (15cm × 20cm) of printed fabric for wings

- 1 piece 9″ × 10″ (22.5cm × 25cm) of craft felt for wings

- 1 piece 1″ × 2″ (2.5cm × 5cm) of craft felt for eyes

- 2 mini buttons for eyes

- 2 buttons for attaching wings

- 1 oval of card stock 1½″ × 1¾″ (3.5cm × 4cm) for base

- 1 pebble for weight

- Stuffing

- A selection of coordinating pearl cotton 8 threads for the appliqué and embroidery

- Sewing thread in a color to match the body parts, suitable for use either in a sewing machine or for hand stitching, for constructing the Swan

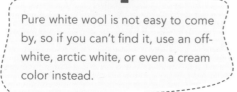

tip

Pure white wool is not easy to come by, so if you can't find it, use an off-white, arctic white, or even a cream color instead.

Read the Basic Instructions (pages 6–27) for more detailed information.

Patterns are on pages 135–136. Trace and cut out the patterns.

BODY

1. From the felted wool, cut 2 bodies (1 and 1 reverse).

2. Construct the body (pages 13–14). Stuff it and add the pebble for weight. Add the card-stock base and attach the felted-wool base.

3. From the first printed fabric, cut 1 chest and base patch.

4. Sew the chest and base patch in place (page 15) using random straight stitches (page 23), making sure the base area is covered completely by the fabric. Add a couple of tucks in the fabric, if need be, to allow it to fit snugly against the Swan's body.

Add tucks in the printed-fabric chest and base patch.

FACE AND BEAK

1. From the second felted wool, cut 2 top beaks (1 and 1 reverse).

2. Place them right sides together and stitch along the edge marked *Center* on the pattern.

3. Open out this beak part and use it as a pattern to cut the bottom of the beak from the third felted wool by pinning them right sides together. Cut out the bottom beak but ignore the V shape at the top of the joined beak and just cut straight across. Stitch along the 2 longer edges to make a point. Turn the beak right side out, using the stuffer stick to poke out the point.

4. Fill the beak with a little stuffing and attach it to the Swan's head using straight stitches. Add 2 straight stitch crosses in a dark color as nostrils on both sides of the beak.

5. From the craft felt, cut 2 eye circles and attach them using the mini buttons (page 8).

tip

Use a very scant ¼″ (0.5cm) seam allowance when stitching the beak seams. Trim the seams to reduce bulk if necessary, especially at the tip. Be gentle when turning and stuffing, so the stitching does not pull out.

WINGS

1. From the craft felt, cut 2 large (1 and 1 reverse) wings and 1 small wing. From the second printed fabric, cut a large wing. From the first printed fabric, cut 1 wing decoration circle.

2. Construct the Swan's left wing from a craft-felt piece (reverse) paired with a printed-fabric piece, wrong sides together, using a blanket stitch (page 22) all the way around the edge. (No stuffing is added.)

3. Layer the left wing by first laying down the craft-felt piece, then the blanket-stitch-edged piece, and then the smaller wing. Top it off with a wing decoration circle, roughly lining up the joining points as marked on the patterns. Pin all the layers together and attach the wing to the Swan's left side with one of the buttons.

4. Stitching through all of the wing layers and also the Swan's body, add 3 long, straight stitches, to anchor the wing further.

5. Repeat Steps 1–4 for the right wing using the following pieces: 2 craft-felt large wings (1 and 1 reverse), 1 printed-fabric large wing (reverse), 1 craft-felt small wing (reverse), and 1 wing decoration circle.

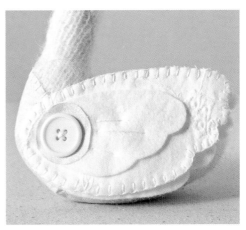

tip

When stuffing the Swan's body, you may find the felted-wool neck twists slightly. Don't worry about this. It will add to the character of the Swan and make it look more lifelike.

duck

Finished size approximately 4½" × 5" (11cm × 12.5cm)

Ducks are amusing little water birds. I don't know any child who doesn't roar with laughter trying to emulate a duck's waddle or quack!

You will need

- 1 piece 5" × 11" (12.5cm × 27.5cm) of felted wool (page 8) for body

- 1 piece 2" × 3½" (5cm × 9cm) of felted wool (page 8) for beak

- 1 piece 5" × 7" (12.5cm × 17.5cm) of printed fabric for the chest and base patch and wings

- 1 piece 4" × 6" (10cm × 15cm) of craft felt for wings

- 1 piece 1" × 2" (2.5cm × 5cm) of craft felt for eyes

- 2 mini buttons for eyes

- 2 buttons to attach wings

- 1 oval of card stock 1¼" × 1½" (3cm × 3.5cm) for base

- 1 pebble for weight

- Stuffing

- A selection of coordinating pearl cotton 8 threads for the appliqué and embroidery

- Sewing thread in a color to match the body parts, suitable for use either in a sewing machine or for hand stitching, for constructing the Duck

Additional for the Duckling Finger Puppet:
- 1 piece 2½" × 6" (6.5cm × 15cm) of craft felt for the body

- 1 piece 1" × 2" (2.5cm × 5cm) of craft felt for the wings

- 1 piece 1" × 1" (2.5cm × 2.5cm) of craft felt for the beak

- 2 mini buttons for the eyes

- A selection of coordinating pearl cotton 8 threads for the embroidery

Additional for the Egg:
- 1 piece 3" × 5" (7.5cm × 12.5cm) of craft felt for the Egg

- A selection of coordinating pearl cotton 8 threads for the embroidery

- Stuffing

Read the Basic Instructions (pages 6–27) for more detailed information.

Patterns are on page 137. Trace and cut out the patterns.

tips

- Since birds' feathers are often mottled in nature, you have a great opportunity here to use a printed felted wool. A stripy or fair isle pattern in soft hues of gray and brown will give a lovely muted effect for a female Duck.

- For a male Duck, use the same pattern with brighter-colored felted wool. Blue or turquoise would work well.

BODY

1. From the felted wool, cut 2 bodies (1 and 1 reverse).

2. Construct the body (pages 13–14). Stuff it and add the pebble for weight. Add the card-stock base and attach the felted-wool base.

3. From the first printed fabric, cut 1 chest and base piece.

4. Sew the chest and base piece in place (page 15) using random straight stitches (page 23), making sure the base area is covered completely by the fabric. Add a couple of tucks in the fabric, if need be, to allow it to fit snugly against the Duck's body, as marked on the pattern.

FACE AND BEAK

1. From the second felted wool, cut 2 beaks.

2. Construct the beak (pages 15–16), leaving the short top edge open. Turn it right side out, using the stuffer stick to poke out the point. Fill it with a little stuffing and attach it to the face with random straight stitches.

3. From the craft felt, cut 2 eye circles and attach them using the mini buttons (page 8).

WINGS

1. From each of the printed fabric and the first craft felt, cut 2 wings (1 and 1 reverse).

2. Construct each wing (page 18) with a printed-fabric piece and a craft-felt piece, using a blanket stitch. Attach a wing to each side of the Duck, fabric side facing outward, with 1 button.

3. Using a thread color that will blend with your chosen printed fabric, add some small straight stitches along the bottom edge of the wing to join it to the Duck's body and create a pocket. (See Tip, page 107.)

duckling finger puppet

1. From the first craft felt, cut 2 bodies (1 and 1 reverse). From the second craft felt, cut 2 wings (1 and 1 reverse). From the third craft felt, cut a beak.

2. On the first body piece, sew on the wing with a few random straight stitches and attach a mini button eye. Take the second body piece, flip it so it is facing the opposite direction of the first, and attach the wing and an eye.

3. Pin the 2 bodies wrong sides together, sandwiching the overlap area (marked on the pattern) of the beak in between. Sew a running stitch (page 24) all the way around, leaving a ¾″ (2cm) gap at the bottom.

egg

1. From the craft felt, cut 2 Eggs.

2. Pin them wrong sides together and stitch around the edge in a blanket stitch (page 22), but before finishing, leave a small gap. Push in a little stuffing with the stuffer stick and continue sewing to close up the gap.

3. Add a few seed stitches (page 25) on both sides of the Egg toward the bottom to create a mottled effect on the shell.

tip

Tuck the Egg and the Duckling Finger Puppet into the pockets created by the wings on the Mother Duck.

kingfisher

Finished size approximately 3″ × 6″ (7.5cm × 15cm)

The kingfisher is a spectacular little bird. The splashes of blue, turquoise, and orange lend themselves perfectly to any craft project, making it a joy to re-create.

You will need

- 1 piece 5″ × 10″ (12.5cm × 25cm) of felted wool (page 8) for body

- 1 piece 3″ × 5″ (7.5cm × 12.5cm) of printed fabric for chest and base patch

- 1 piece 3″ × 6″ (7.5cm × 15cm) of printed fabric for wings

- 1 piece 2″ × 3″ (5cm × 7.5cm) of craft felt for beak

- 1 piece 3″ × 6″ (7.5cm × 15cm) of craft felt for wings and inner eye

- 1 piece 2″ × 2″ (5cm × 5cm) of craft felt for outer eye

- 2 mini buttons for eyes

- 2 buttons to attach wings

- 1 oval of card stock 1″ × 1½″ (2.5cm × 3cm) for the base

- 1 pebble for weight

- Stuffing

- A selection of coordinating pearl cotton 8 threads for the appliqué and embroidery

- Sewing thread in a color to match the body parts, suitable for use either in a sewing machine or for hand stitching, for constructing the Kingfisher

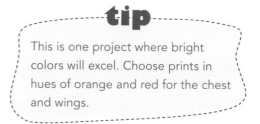

tip

This is one project where bright colors will excel. Choose prints in hues of orange and red for the chest and wings.

Read the Basic Instructions (pages 6–27) for more detailed information.

Patterns are on page 138. Trace and cut out the patterns.

BODY

1. From the felted wool, cut 2 bodies (1 and 1 reverse).

2. Construct the body (pages 13–14). Stuff it and add the pebble for weight. Add the card-stock base and attach the felted-wool base.

3. From the first printed fabric, cut 1 chest and base patch.

4. Sew the chest and base patch in place (page 15) using random straight stitches (page 23), making sure the base area is covered completely by the fabric. If need be, add a couple of tucks in the fabric, as marked on the pattern, to allow it to fit snugly against the Kingfisher's body.

EYES AND BEAK

1. From the third craft felt, cut 2 outer eye pieces. From the second craft felt, cut 2 inner eyes.

2. Stitch an outer eye in place on the side of the Kingfisher's head with random straight stitches (page 23). Place an inner eye on top and anchor it in place by sewing a mini button in the center. Repeat on the other side of the head for the other eye.

3. From the first craft felt, cut 2 beaks. Place 1 on top of the other and join them by stitching up the middle in a running stitch if sewing by hand (page 24) or a straight stitch (page 26) if sewing by machine. Trim as desired. Attach the beak to the face using straight stitches.

WINGS

1. From each of the second printed fabric and the second craft felt, cut 2 wings (1 and 1 reverse from each fabric).

2. Construct the wings (page 18) using a printed-fabric piece and a craft-felt piece, wrong sides together, using a blanket stitch all around. Attach each wing to a side of the Kingfisher, with the fabric side facing outward, with 1 button.

FEATHERS

Add some straight stitches (page 23) to the Kingfisher's body as feathers. (They run down the bird's back.)

bulrush/cattail

In the UK, it's a bulrush; in America, it's a cattail. These striking plants are found at the edges of ponds, streams, rivers, and lakes and are surprisingly simple to make using a few raw materials.

Finished size approximately 1˝ × 18˝ (2.5cm × 45cm)

Read the Basic Instructions (pages 6–27) for more detailed information.

Patterns are on page 139. Trace and cut out the patterns.

tips

• You could make 2 or 3 Bulrushes to display in a vase.

• Don't worry about any fraying of the fabric strips on the stem; this will add a natural quality to the fabric.

You will need

• 1 piece 4˝ × 5˝ (10cm × 12.5cm) of felted wool (page 8) for top

• 1 piece 2˝ × 3˝ (5cm × 7.5cm) of craft felt for spike

• 1 strip roughly ½˝ × 36˝ (1.5cm × 90cm) of printed fabric to wrap around stem

• 1 piece 36˝ (90cm) of garden wire (page 10)

• Stuffing

• A selection of coordinating pearl cotton 8 threads for the embroidery

• Sewing thread in a color to match the body parts, suitable for use either in a sewing machine or for hand stitching, for constructing the Bulrush

• Gluestick (page 7)

STEM

Bend the length of garden wire into thirds and, holding 1 end, cover the wire with glue from the gluestick. Beginning at the bottom, tuck one end of the strip of printed fabric between the wire strands and wrap it round and round, covering the wire. Move up the wire as you go and add more glue if needed. Rub some glue onto the outside fabric to hold down any loose areas if needed. The glue will dry clear, so it will not spoil the fabric. If you need more fabric, add in a new strip, again by tucking the end in between the wire strands. Continue until all the wire is covered. Anchor the end of the final strip of fabric with some more glue and trim it of any excess. Let it dry.

BULRUSH

1. From the felted wool, cut 2 Bulrushes.

2. Place the 2 Bulrush felted wool pieces right sides together. Stitch all around, by hand using a backstitch (page 23) or by straight stitch using a machine (page 26), and leave a gap at the bottom. Turn the body right side out and stuff.

3. Poke one end of the stem into the bottom gap and add stitches to close the gap, making sure the needle also goes through the wrapped and glued fabric.

4. From the craft felt, cut 2 spikes.

5. Place 1 spike on top of the other and stitch a running stitch (page 24) if sewing by hand or by machine down the center through both layers. Attach the spike to the top of the Bulrush, using straight stitches.

6. Add a bit of texture to the Bulrush with some embroidery—horizontal straight stitches on one side, and some vertical straight stitches on the other.

DISPLAYING THE KINGFISHER AND BULRUSH

Bend the bottom 7″ (17cm) of the stem into a circle to form a base, making sure the rest of the stem with the Bulrush stands straight. The Bulrush may not stand by itself, but if you set the Kingfisher within the circular base, the two will sit nicely together.

dragonfly

Finished size approximately 3¾″ × 6½″ (9cm × 16cm)

Dragonflies have such a unique way of flying because of their double wings that they seem to dance through the air. Their iridescent coloring makes them an appealing insect for many areas of art and craft to draw inspiration from.

You will need

- 1 piece 4″ × 5″ (10cm × 12.5cm) of felted wool (page 8) for body

- 2 pieces 4″ × 6″ (10cm × 15cm) of printed fabric for wings (2 different fabrics suggested)

- 2 buttons for the eyes

- 1 piece 4″ × 6″ (10cm × 15cm) of interfacing (page 8) for wings

- Stuffing

- Brown pearl cotton 5 for the legs

- A selection of coordinating pearl cotton 8 threads for the embroidery

- Sewing thread in a color to match the body parts, suitable for use either in a sewing machine or for hand stitching, for constructing the Dragonfly

Read the Basic Instructions (pages 6–27) for more detailed information.

Patterns are on page 139. Trace and cut out the patterns.

BODY

1. From felted wool, cut 2 bodies.

2. Place the 2 Dragonfly body felted-wool pieces right sides together. Stitch all around by hand using a backstitch (page 23) or a straight stitch by machine (page 26), leaving a gap at the bottom. Turn the body right side out and stuff.

NOTE

Since the Dragonfly is so small, you will need to sew as close to the edge as you can. Turn the body right side out, using the stuffer stick to poke out the point, and stuff. Stitch the gap with a whipstitch (page 26) in a sewing thread that matches the body color.

WINGS

1. From 1 of the printed fabrics, cut 4 top wings (2 and 2 reverse). From the other printed fabric, cut 4 bottom wings (2 and 2 reverse). From interfacing, cut 2 of each wing.

2. Layer each wing with matching printed-fabric top and bottom, wrong sides together, with the interfacing sandwiched in between. Sew all the way around ¼″ (0.5cm) in from the edge of each wing, using a running stitch (page 24) if sewing by hand or a straight stitch (page 26) if sewing on a machine.

3. Attach 1 of the top wings and 1 of the bottom wings to each side of the Dragonfly using random straight stitches (page 23).

Underside of wings

LEGS, ANTENNAE, AND EYES

1. Using the pearl cotton 5, add 6 legs (page 20) to the underside (the side where the bottom wings are attached).

2. Turn the Dragonfly over and add 2 antennae using the pearl cotton 8 (page 20).

3. Add the 2 button eyes.

4. Finish by adding an extra length of thread (pearl cotton 8 will do) as a hanging thread. Anchor it to the Dragonfly in the center of the body between the top wings so it hangs straight when held in the air. Decide how long you want the hanger to be, fold over the other end of the thread, and tie a knot to make a loop.

patterns

Fox patterns

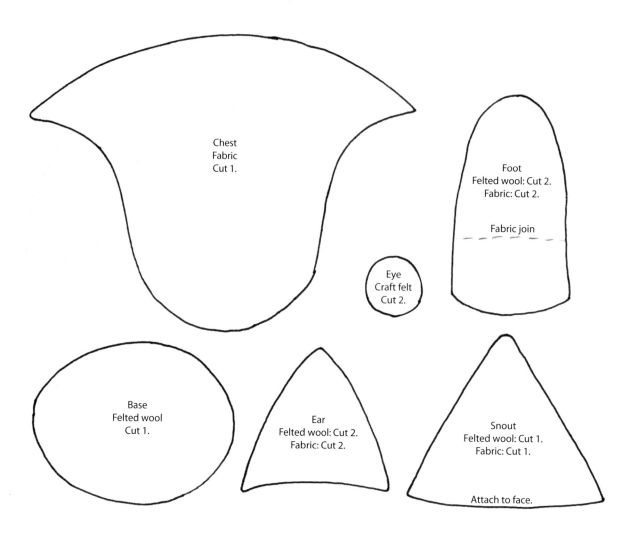

Chest
Fabric
Cut 1.

Foot
Felted wool: Cut 2.
Fabric: Cut 2.

Fabric join

Eye
Craft felt
Cut 2.

Base
Felted wool
Cut 1.

Ear
Felted wool: Cut 2.
Fabric: Cut 2.

Snout
Felted wool: Cut 1.
Fabric: Cut 1.

Attach to face.

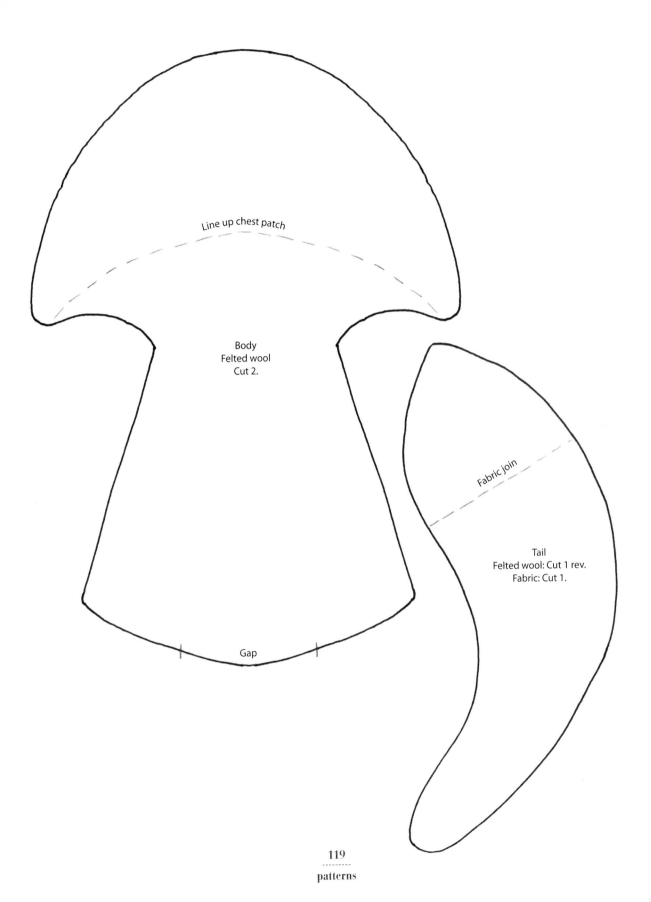

Line up chest patch

Body
Felted wool
Cut 2.

Gap

Fabric join

Tail
Felted wool: Cut 1 rev.
Fabric: Cut 1.

Rabbit patterns

Male Body
Felted wool
Cut 2 (1 + 1 rev.).

Female Tummy
Fabric
Cut 1.

Tie
Craft felt
Cut 1.

Gap

Flower
Craft felt
Cut 1.

Male Tummy
Fabric
Cut 1.

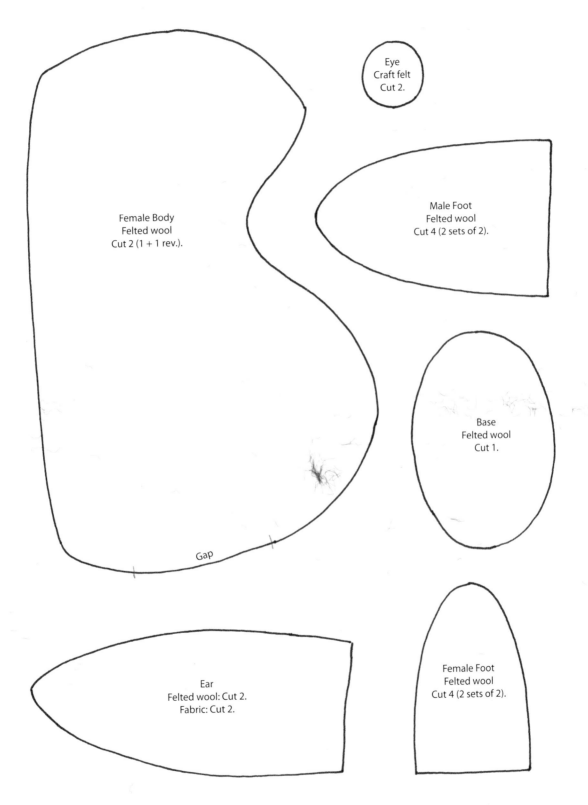

Eye
Craft felt
Cut 2.

Female Body
Felted wool
Cut 2 (1 + 1 rev.).

Male Foot
Felted wool
Cut 4 (2 sets of 2).

Base
Felted wool
Cut 1.

Gap

Ear
Felted wool: Cut 2.
Fabric: Cut 2.

Female Foot
Felted wool
Cut 4 (2 sets of 2).

Baby Rabbit and Carrot patterns

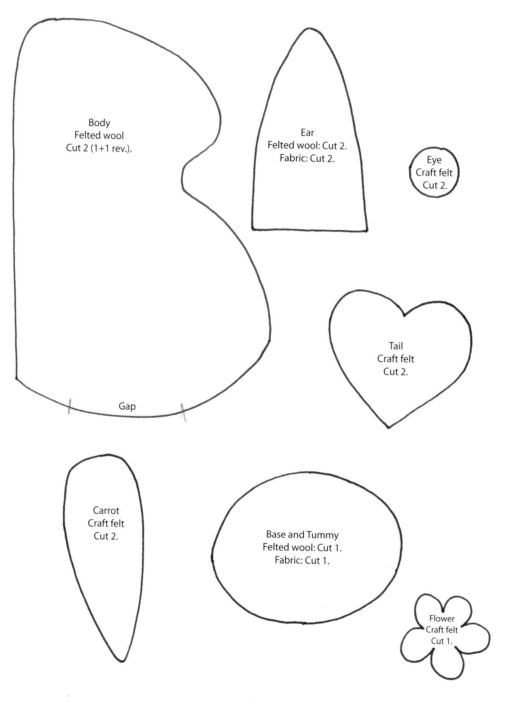

Body
Felted wool
Cut 2 (1+1 rev.).

Gap

Ear
Felted wool: Cut 2.
Fabric: Cut 2.

Eye
Craft felt
Cut 2.

Tail
Craft felt
Cut 2.

Carrot
Craft felt
Cut 2.

Base and Tummy
Felted wool: Cut 1.
Fabric: Cut 1.

Flower
Craft felt
Cut 1.

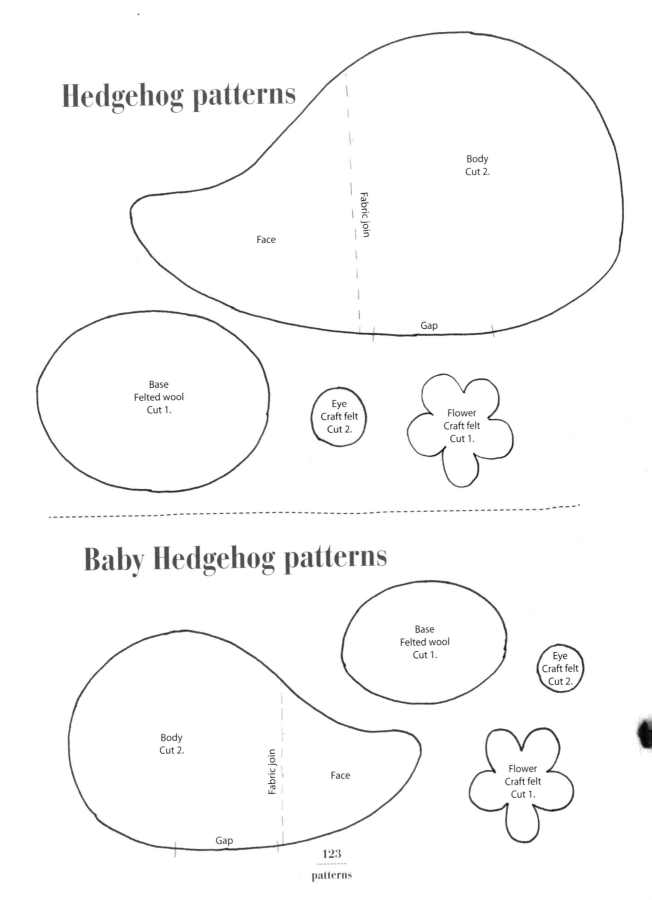

Hedgehog patterns

Body
Cut 2.

Face

Fabric join

Gap

Base
Felted wool
Cut 1.

Eye
Craft felt
Cut 2.

Flower
Craft felt
Cut 1.

Baby Hedgehog patterns

Base
Felted wool
Cut 1.

Eye
Craft felt
Cut 2.

Body
Cut 2.

Fabric join

Face

Flower
Craft felt
Cut 1.

Gap

Robin patterns

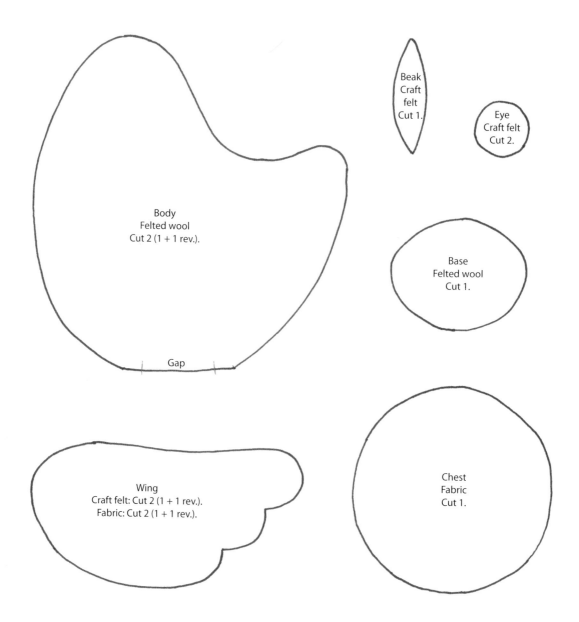

Body
Felted wool
Cut 2 (1 + 1 rev.).

Gap

Beak
Craft
felt
Cut 1.

Eye
Craft felt
Cut 2.

Base
Felted wool
Cut 1.

Wing
Craft felt: Cut 2 (1 + 1 rev.).
Fabric: Cut 2 (1 + 1 rev.).

Chest
Fabric
Cut 1.

Robin Ornament patterns

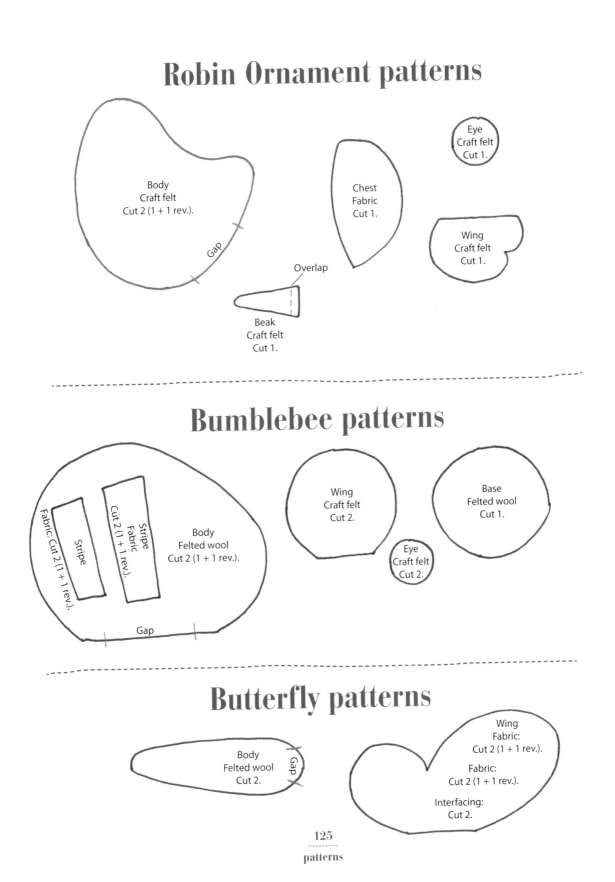

Body
Craft felt
Cut 2 (1 + 1 rev.).

Gap

Chest
Fabric
Cut 1.

Eye
Craft felt
Cut 1.

Wing
Craft felt
Cut 1.

Overlap

Beak
Craft felt
Cut 1.

Bumblebee patterns

Fabric: Cut 2 (1 + 1 rev.).

Stripe

Stripe
Fabric
Cut 2 (1 + 1 rev.).

Body
Felted wool
Cut 2 (1 + 1 rev.).

Gap

Wing
Craft felt
Cut 2.

Eye
Craft felt
Cut 2.

Base
Felted wool
Cut 1.

Butterfly patterns

Body
Felted wool
Cut 2.

Gap

Wing
Fabric:
Cut 2 (1 + 1 rev.).

Fabric:
Cut 2 (1 + 1 rev.).

Interfacing:
Cut 2.

Squirrel patterns

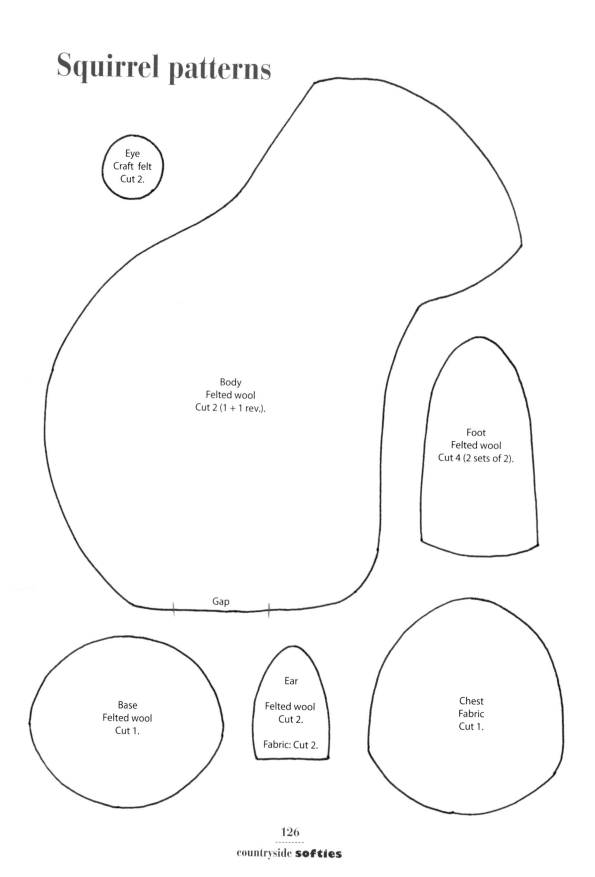

Eye
Craft felt
Cut 2.

Body
Felted wool
Cut 2 (1 + 1 rev.).

Foot
Felted wool
Cut 4 (2 sets of 2).

Gap

Base
Felted wool
Cut 1.

Ear

Felted wool
Cut 2.

Fabric: Cut 2.

Chest
Fabric
Cut 1.

Badger patterns

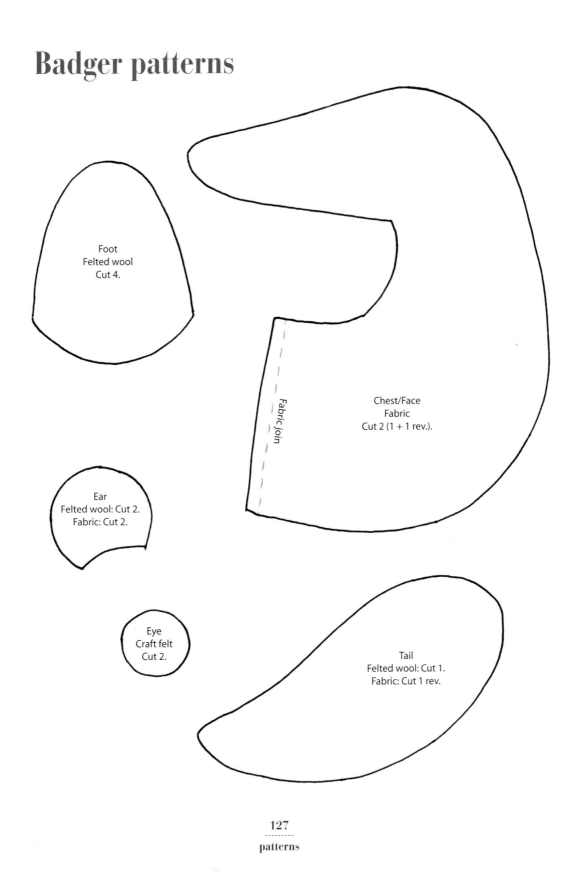

Foot
Felted wool
Cut 4.

Chest/Face
Fabric
Cut 2 (1 + 1 rev.).

Fabric join

Ear
Felted wool: Cut 2.
Fabric: Cut 2.

Eye
Craft felt
Cut 2.

Tail
Felted wool: Cut 1.
Fabric: Cut 1 rev.

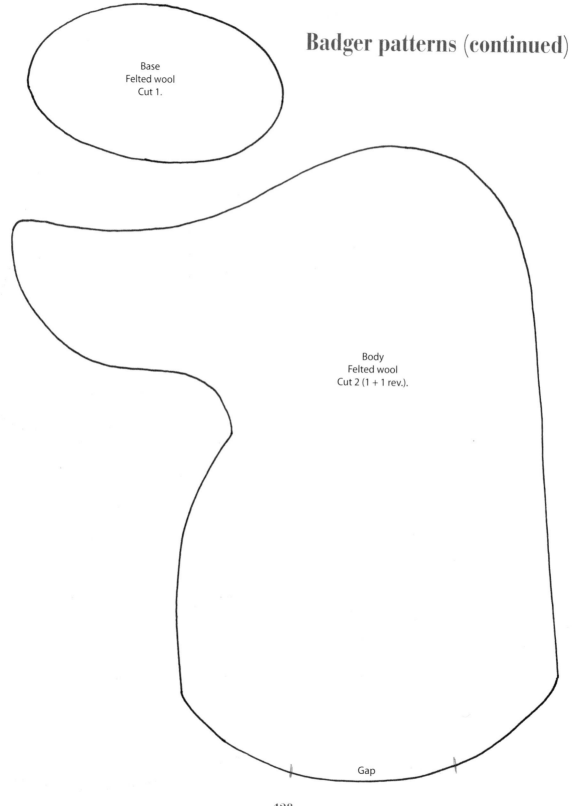

Base
Felted wool
Cut 1.

Body
Felted wool
Cut 2 (1 + 1 rev.).

Gap

Owl patterns

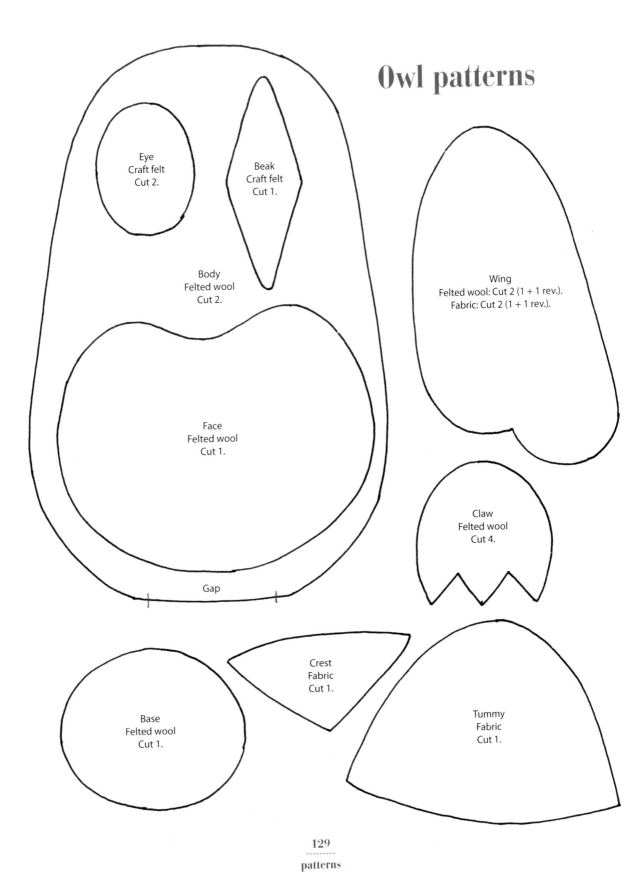

Eye
Craft felt
Cut 2.

Beak
Craft felt
Cut 1.

Body
Felted wool
Cut 2.

Wing
Felted wool: Cut 2 (1 + 1 rev.).
Fabric: Cut 2 (1 + 1 rev.).

Face
Felted wool
Cut 1.

Gap

Claw
Felted wool
Cut 4.

Base
Felted wool
Cut 1.

Crest
Fabric
Cut 1.

Tummy
Fabric
Cut 1.

Baby Owl patterns

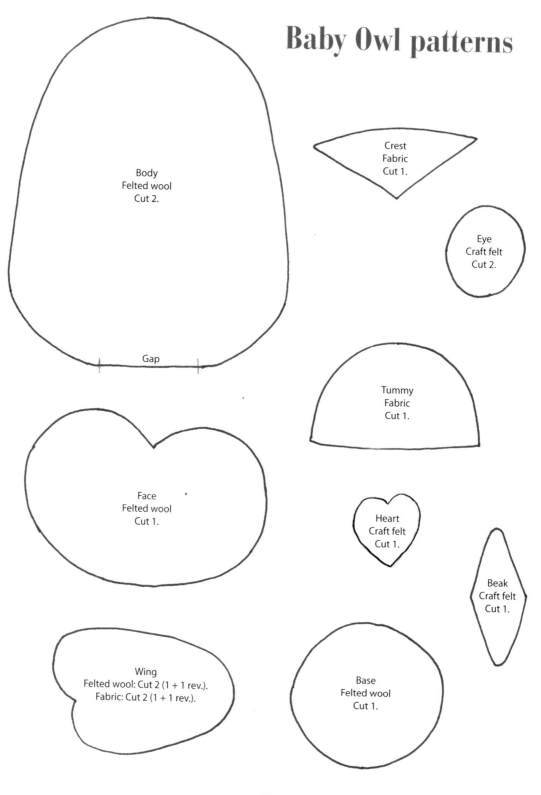

Body
Felted wool
Cut 2.

Crest
Fabric
Cut 1.

Eye
Craft felt
Cut 2.

Gap

Tummy
Fabric
Cut 1.

Face
Felted wool
Cut 1.

Heart
Craft felt
Cut 1.

Beak
Craft felt
Cut 1.

Wing
Felted wool: Cut 2 (1 + 1 rev.).
Fabric: Cut 2 (1 + 1 rev.).

Base
Felted wool
Cut 1.

Mouse patterns

Body
Felted wool
Cut 2 (1 + 1 rev.).

Bow Tie
Craft felt: Cut 1.

Flower
Craft felt
Cut 1.

Gap

Tail
Felted wool: Cut 1.
Fabric: Cut 1 rev.

Eye
Craft felt
Cut 2.

Ear
Felted wool: Cut 2.
Fabric: Cut 2.

Base and Tummy
Felted wool: Cut 1.
Fabric: Cut 1.

Heart
Craft felt
Cut 1.

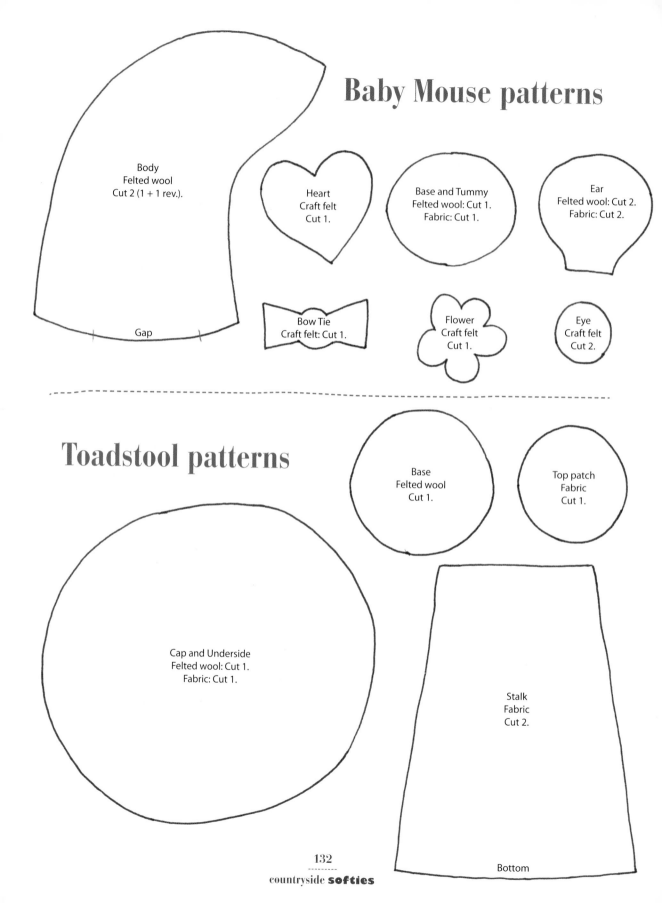

Baby Mouse patterns

Body
Felted wool
Cut 2 (1 + 1 rev.).

Gap

Heart
Craft felt
Cut 1.

Base and Tummy
Felted wool: Cut 1.
Fabric: Cut 1.

Ear
Felted wool: Cut 2.
Fabric: Cut 2.

Bow Tie
Craft felt: Cut 1.

Flower
Craft felt
Cut 1.

Eye
Craft felt
Cut 2.

Toadstool patterns

Base
Felted wool
Cut 1.

Top patch
Fabric
Cut 1.

Cap and Underside
Felted wool: Cut 1.
Fabric: Cut 1.

Stalk
Fabric
Cut 2.

Bottom

Otter and Fish patterns

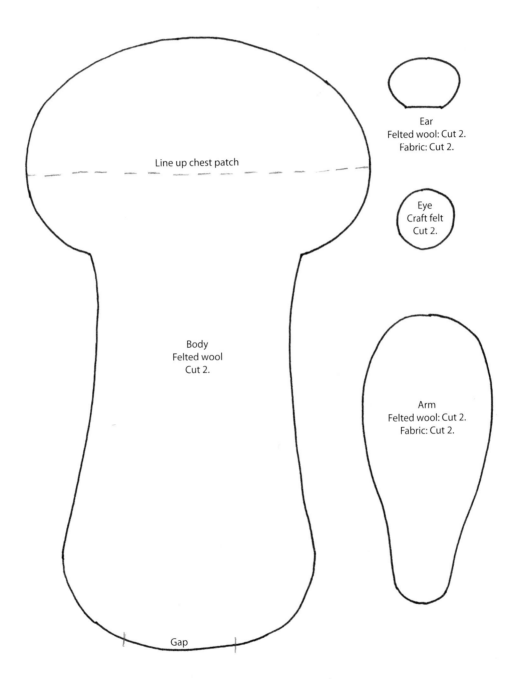

Ear
Felted wool: Cut 2.
Fabric: Cut 2.

Eye
Craft felt
Cut 2.

Line up chest patch

Body
Felted wool
Cut 2.

Arm
Felted wool: Cut 2.
Fabric: Cut 2.

Gap

Otter and Fish patterns (continued)

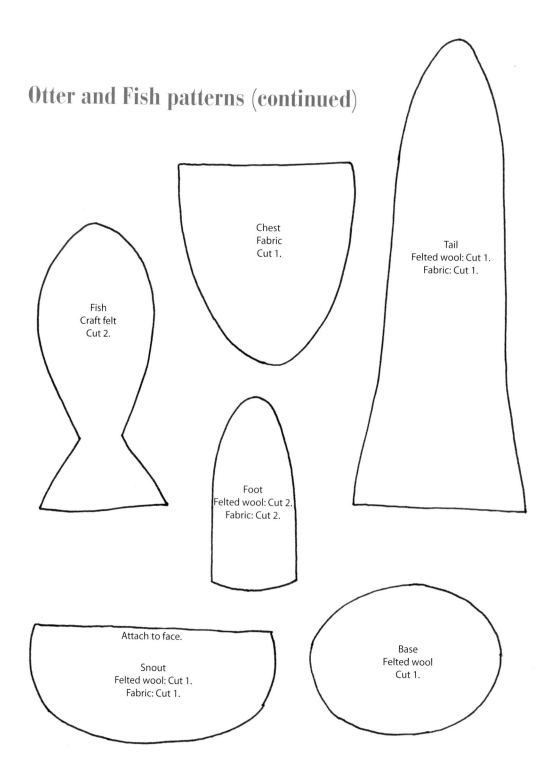

Fish
Craft felt
Cut 2.

Chest
Fabric
Cut 1.

Tail
Felted wool: Cut 1.
Fabric: Cut 1.

Foot
Felted wool: Cut 2.
Fabric: Cut 2.

Attach to face.

Snout
Felted wool: Cut 1.
Fabric: Cut 1.

Base
Felted wool
Cut 1.

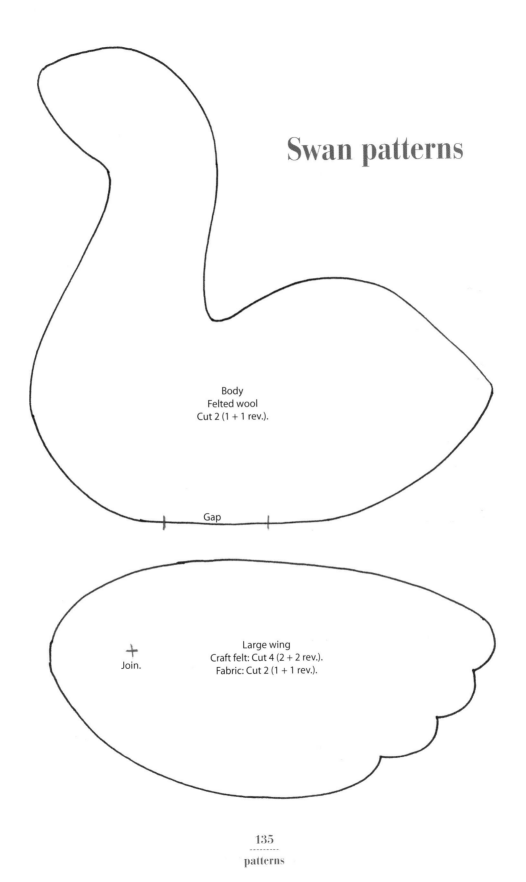

Swan patterns

Body
Felted wool
Cut 2 (1 + 1 rev.).

Gap

Large wing
Craft felt: Cut 4 (2 + 2 rev.).
Fabric: Cut 2 (1 + 1 rev.).

+
Join.

Swan patterns (continued)

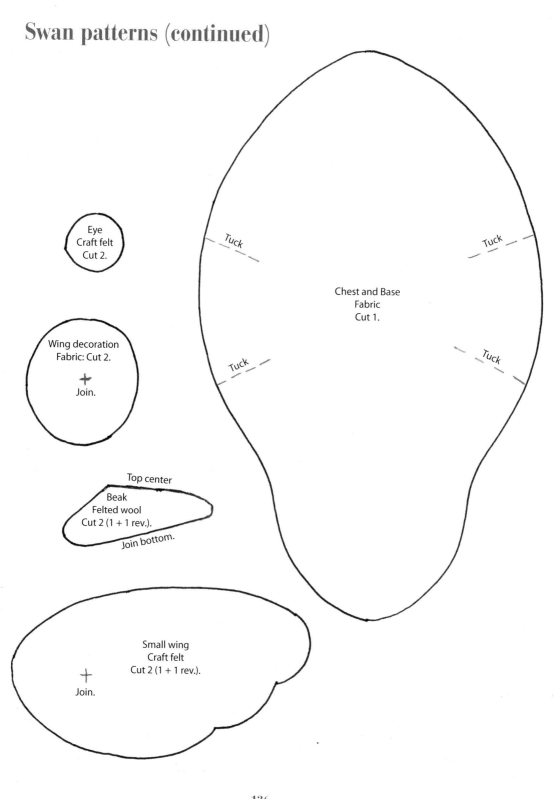

Eye
Craft felt
Cut 2.

Wing decoration
Fabric: Cut 2.

+
Join.

Chest and Base
Fabric
Cut 1.

Tuck

Tuck

Tuck

Tuck

Top center

Beak
Felted wool
Cut 2 (1 + 1 rev.).

Join bottom.

Small wing
Craft felt
Cut 2 (1 + 1 rev.).

+
Join.

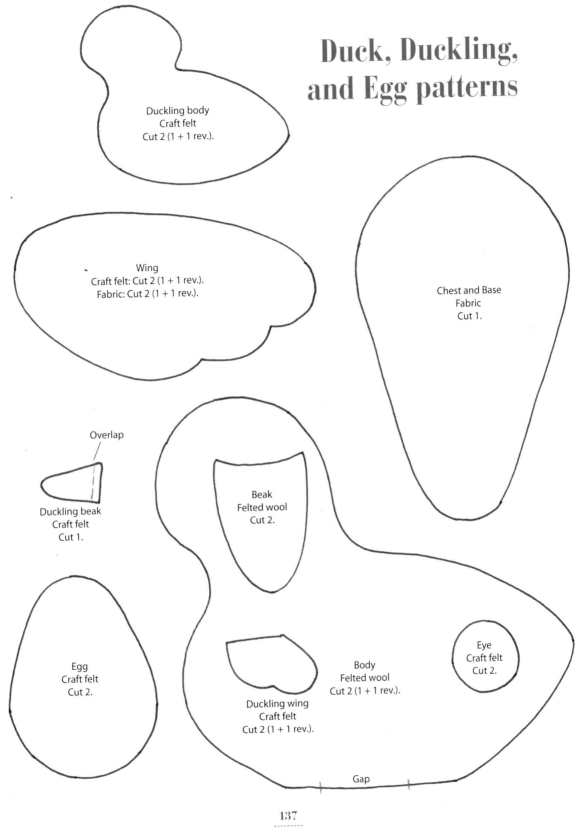

Duck, Duckling, and Egg patterns

Duckling body
Craft felt
Cut 2 (1 + 1 rev.).

Wing
Craft felt: Cut 2 (1 + 1 rev.).
Fabric: Cut 2 (1 + 1 rev.).

Chest and Base
Fabric
Cut 1.

Overlap

Duckling beak
Craft felt
Cut 1.

Beak
Felted wool
Cut 2.

Egg
Craft felt
Cut 2.

Body
Felted wool
Cut 2 (1 + 1 rev.).

Eye
Craft felt
Cut 2.

Duckling wing
Craft felt
Cut 2 (1 + 1 rev.).

Gap

137

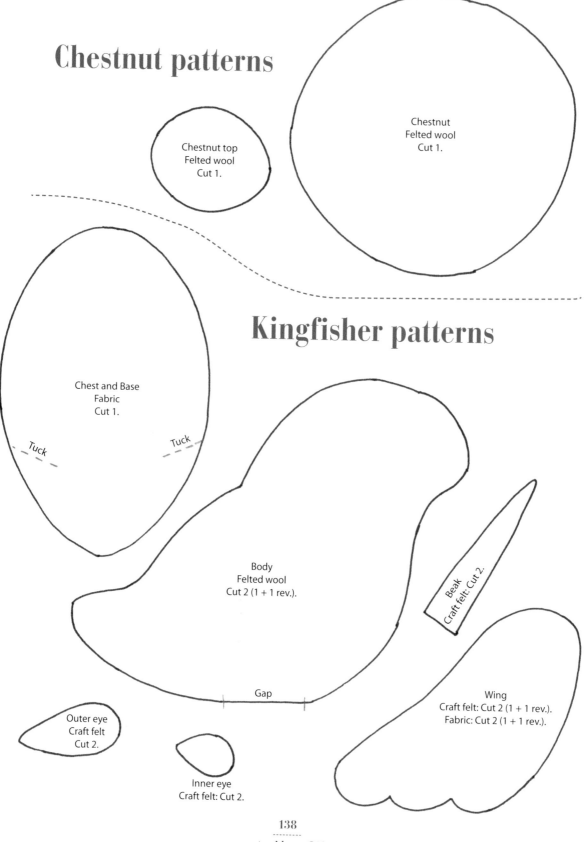

Chestnut patterns

Chestnut top
Felted wool
Cut 1.

Chestnut
Felted wool
Cut 1.

Kingfisher patterns

Chest and Base
Fabric
Cut 1.

Tuck

Tuck

Body
Felted wool
Cut 2 (1 + 1 rev.).

Beak
Craft felt: Cut 2.

Gap

Wing
Craft felt: Cut 2 (1 + 1 rev.).
Fabric: Cut 2 (1 + 1 rev.).

Outer eye
Craft felt
Cut 2.

Inner eye
Craft felt: Cut 2.

Dragonfly patterns

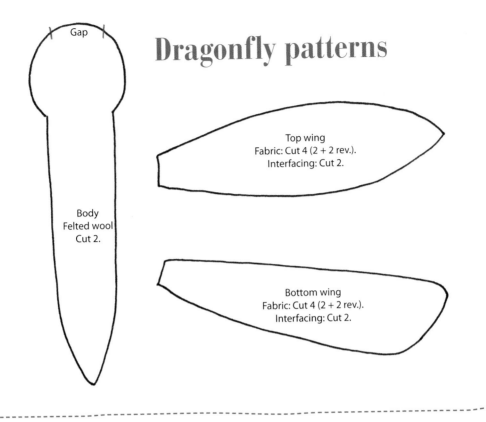

Gap

Body
Felted wool
Cut 2.

Top wing
Fabric: Cut 4 (2 + 2 rev.).
Interfacing: Cut 2.

Bottom wing
Fabric: Cut 4 (2 + 2 rev.).
Interfacing: Cut 2.

Bulrush/Cattail patterns

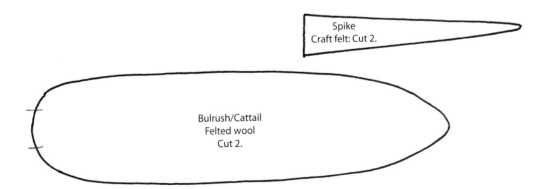

Spike
Craft felt: Cut 2.

Bulrush/Cattail
Felted wool
Cut 2.

resources

woolens for felting

Goodwill
Check www.goodwill.org for your nearest store location.

eBay
www.ebay.com

Resweater
www.artfire.com/users/Resweater

fabrics and craft felt

Superbuzzy
1932 Eastman Avenue #106
Ventura, CA 93003
(805) 644-4143
www.superbuzzy.com

Purl Patchwork
459 Broome Street
New York, NY 10013
(212) 420-8796
www.purlsoho.com

fabrics

Reprodepot
116 Pleasant Street
Easthampton, MA 01027
(postal address only)
www.reprodepot.com

Sew Mama Sew
P.O. Box 1127
Beaverton, OR 97075
(503) 380-3584
www.sewmamasew.com/store

craft felt

Felt-o-rama
9716-B Rea Road #150
Charlotte, NC 28277
(888) 393-4050
www.feltorama.com

notions & supplies

Jo-Ann Fabric and Craft Stores
5555 Darrow Road
Hudson, OH 44236
www.joann.com

Pearl Cotton embroidery thread
Coats & Clark
P.O. Box 12229
Greenville, SC 29612
(800) 648-1479
www.coatsandclark.com

Mini Buttons
Dress It Up c/o Jesse James Beads
950 Jennings Street
Bethlehem, PA 18017
www.jessejamesbeads.com

Buttons Galore & More
250 Pinedge Drive
West Berlin, NJ 08091
(856) 753-6700
www.buttonsgaloreandmore.com

stuffing

Mountain Mist
2551 Crescentville Road
Cincinnati, OH 45241
(513) 326-3912
www.stearnstextiles.com

blogging

For a designer of any kind, in this day and age, an online web presence will be a useful commodity. There are many ways of building a website—ranging from writing the HTML code yourself to employing a third party or purchasing software that has a ready-made template to personalize. Blogging is another way and has the advantage of getting you online quickly and easily.

Setting up a blog is relatively painless. The pre-designed templates can be used as they are or custom-ized in your own choice of colors and layout. Spend a bit of time putting together a blog banner, something intriguing to draw readers in and make them want to know more. As your blog readership grows, post regularly—once a week, twice a week, it's up to you. Visit other blogs and comment and begin discus-sions about things you have seen that you like; blogging is about participating in a community. It is a reap what you sow (or sew in this case!) experience.

blogging resources

Blogger
Run by Google, Blogger is simple, fun, and very user friendly.

www.blogger.com

Typepad
This platform does have a small monthly fee, but it offers many additional features in return.

www.typepad.com

Wordpress
Wordpress is free, and the new incarnation (.com as opposed to .org) now comes with web hosting included.

www.wordpress.com

Before choosing which to go for, have a look around the Internet at the blogs you like to visit and that you like the aesthetics and layout. All three have forums on their websites that can help with any questions and troubleshooting you may have.

Lucykate Crafts … (http://lucykatecrafts.blogspot.com)

photography

A key factor in any design blog is imagery. Readers want and need to see what it is you are posting about. If you don't already have a camera, get one. Take time to get to know your camera; it will be worth it in order to get the most out of any shot you take. When photographing textiles, the most important elements are texture and color. The best tool for getting these right is a steady hand. If your hands aren't steady, invest in a tripod. And use natural light—and plenty of it!

But most important of all, have fun and join in!

about the author

It was a visit to an exhibition of historical embroidery that began to evoke the notion of a career in textiles for Amy Adams. After studying for a degree in weaving and embroidery at De Montford University in the United Kingdom, Amy began a twelve-year stint as a professional designer, creating counted cross-stitch, tapestry, and embroidery kits. As the product range diversified, she began to engage in designing kits encompassing paper crafts, patchwork, soft toys, and rag dolls. It was the transition of fabrics and embroidery from two-dimensional to three-dimensional that captured her imagination the most, and after a family relocation, an opportunity arose to begin following this new path.

Amy's website, Lucykate Crafts (www.lucykatecrafts.co.uk), began as a channel for new ideas and has grown into a busy and resourceful site in the online crafting community. Amy's softie designs are showcased there, as well as being featured in many crafting magazines and books, both in the U.K. and the U.S.A.

Amy lives in a small village within the county of Rutland, UK, with her portrait painter husband and their two children.

stashBOOKS

fabric arts for a handmade lifestyle

If you're craving beautiful authenticity in a time of mass-production...Stash Books is for you. Stash Books is a new line of how-to books celebrating fabric arts for a handmade lifestyle. Backed by C&T Publishing's solid reputation for quality, Stash Books will inspire you with contemporary designs, clear and simple instructions, and engaging photography.

www.stashbooks.com